THE WILMINGTON GIANT

THE WILMINGTON GIANT

The Quest for a Lost Myth

RODNEY CASTLEDEN

Illustrated by the author

TURNSTONE PRESS LIMITED
Wellingborough, Northamptonshire

First published 1983

British Library Cataloguing in Publication Data

Castleden, Rodney
   The Wilmington giant.
   1. Long Man of Wilmington
   I. Title
   942.22'5   DA690.W/

   ISBN 0-85500-184-4
   ISBN 0-85500-185-2 Pbk

*Turnstone Press is part of the
Thorsons Publishing Group*

Printed and bound in Great Britain

CONTENTS

LIST OF ILLUSTRATIONS

Page

On one side of these hills is a curious representation of the figure of a man in the different tincture of the grass. The length of the figure is 240 feet; and each hand grasped a scythe and rake in a parallel direction with the body; but these latter are not visible . . . This, no doubt, was the amusement of some idle Monk belonging to the neighbouring cell. It is formed by a pavement of bricks underneath the turf which gives it this difference of colour. In time of snow it is still more visible.

From *The Topographer*, Volume 3, by E. Brydges and S. Shaw: 'Excursion from Lewes to Eastbourne, in Sussex, 9 November 1790'. The earliest known published account of the Wilmington Giant.

To Libby, Rose, Sally, Karen, Penny and
Clare, for times remembered
and times that might have been.

ACKNOWLEDGEMENTS

Many friends have assisted in the preparation of this book, often without knowing it. As they have walked with me in the Downs, sharing an experience of landscape, they have helped significantly in the development of the ideas that follow. In particular, I have to thank Susan Fisher, Margaret Hunt, Tia Kuchmy and Sister Renate, C.H.N., for coming with me into the hills and making the pleasure of discovery more real. I also have to thank Margaret Hunt, Jane Skinner and Jill Ingham for reading the manuscript and making some useful suggestions for improvements.

On a different level, I should like to thank A. H. Collins, my English master long ago, for insisting that I must substantiate arguments with evidence, and Robin Ruffell, for reminding me intermittently from schooldays onwards to follow my own inward voice. The ideas in this book have remote origins, widely separated in space and time. Some are doubtless unconscious and therefore untraceable. With hindsight, I can see that two specific experiences have had a profound background influence on the gestation of the book. One was the visit I made to the New Grange passage grave in the mid-1960s, when it was being excavated. I was fortunate enough to be shown into the tomb by Professor Michael O'Kelly, the archaeologist leading the dig, and I was very struck by his excitement at what he was discovering, as well as by the mysterious megaliths with their urgent yet indecipherable inscriptions. Another key experience occurred at about the same time: reading Jung's *Symbols of Transformation*.

The lines from *Four Quartets* by T. S. Eliot are reprinted by permission of Faber and Faber Ltd. The lines from 'Hurrahing in Harvest' are reproduced from *The Poems of Gerard Manley Hopkins*, edited by Gardner and MacKenzie and published by Oxford University Press for the Society of Jesus. The plate of the Midsummer Giant is reproduced by permission of the Salisbury and South Wiltshire Museum; that of the Wicker Giant by permission of the British Library. The remaining photographs and line drawings are my own.

Lastly, I should like to thank the Department of the Environment and Mrs Gwynne-Longland, the owner of Windover Hill, for granting me permission to begin essential conservation work on Windover Long Mound. I hope that one effect of this book may be to intensify awareness of the need to conserve ancient monuments, and indeed to conserve such sites even when they appear unremarkable.

R.C., Newhaven, 1983.

1. BEGINNINGS

*Though I have now travelled the Sussex Downs upwards of thirty years,
yet I still investigate that chain of majestic mountains with fresh
admiration year by year, and I think I see new beauties each time I
traverse it . . . For my own part, I think there is something peculiarly
sweet and amusing in the shapely-figured aspect of chalk hills, in
preference to those of stone, which are rugged, broken, abrupt and
shapeless. Perhaps I may be singular in my opinion, but I never
contemplate these mountains without thinking I perceive somewhat
analogous to growth in their gentle swellings and smooth fungus-like
protuberances, their fluted sides and regular hollows and slopes, that
carry at once the air of vegetative dilatation and expansion: or was there
ever a time when the calcareous masses were thrown into fermentation
. . . by some plastic power, and so made to swell and heave their broad
backs into the sky, so much above the less animated clay of the wild
below?*

Gilbert White, *The Natural History of Selborne*, Letter 56.

SPEEDWELL, THYME AND TIPPETT

For as long as I can remember, I have been drawn to the summits of
the South Downs and the woodlands of the Weald below. It is
perhaps surprising that in my boyhood I was altogether unaware of
the silent figure of the Wilmington Giant, or Long Man of
Wilmington, who reclines in a hollow of the Downs and looks out
across the Weald. But once I had seen the Giant my curiosity about
his origins grew steadily. The more I read, the deeper the mystery
became.

The search for the Giant's origins inevitably involved burrowing into the historical and archaeological journals relating to the area, and I spent some long and fascinating days leafing through foxed and dusty volumes. The unexpected bonus was the glorious summer that was spent walking in the hills, exploring the sites that might prove to be connected with the Giant and the people who made him. It was a profoundly rewarding experience that taught me a great deal about the downland landscape. Two personal discoveries that I value highly are the Priory Mount in Lewes and Juggs' Road, the little-known but very beautiful prehistoric trackway leading from Brighton over the hills to Lewes.

I also became aware of the neglect and vandalism that have afflicted many important sites. The prehistoric earthworks on the summit of Windover Hill and at the Whitehawk neolithic camp are being damaged by motorcycle scrambling. The sites have been given no protection from these onslaughts and turf and soil are being ripped unceremoniously from both sites. Such vandalism is not new. It was reported in the Sussex County Magazine of 1939 that five youths were found guilty at Hailsham of wilful damage to the Long Man by pulling bricks from the outline and hurling them down the hill; they were fined thirty shillings each (Anon., 1939). The more formal, official and adult vandalism of the past had more serious effects. A large slice of the Whitehawk camp was completely destroyed by the creation of Brighton Race Course, and the remainder damaged by allotments and roadmaking. The Mount in Lewes has likewise been partially demolished to make room for a bowling green. It is sad that sites of such antiquity, importance and potential beauty should be allowed to suffer in this way. Even the Long Man himself has suffered a degree of neglect, as witnessed in the grossly inadequate restoration that was undertaken, in haste, in 1874 (see Chapter 2).

My walks in the Downs incorporated a survey of the topography and a mental review of the mystery of the Giant's origins. 'Giant theories' seem to rise like an intoxicating vapour from both the literature and the landscape. As I walked, a single piece of music followed me wherever I went: Tippett's 'Fantasia Concertante on a Theme of Corelli'. The dense, wreathing texture of the string orchestras seemed to have been woven out of the densely organic downland turf, with its birdsfoot trefoil, viper's bugloss, ragwort, agrimony, field madder, speedwell and thyme. The solo violins seemed to be a perfect distillation of lark song. Later, the writing of

Plate 1.   The Long Man as he is today. The restored, bricked outline of the Wilmington Giant as seen from the track at the foot of the escarpment.

the book was sustained by the same inward sounds; it is to the writer of that music that I owe the greatest debt.

THE ANCIENT LANDSCAPE

The origin of the Giant marked on the hill side at Wilmington, near Eastbourne, has been the subject of speculation for two centuries at least, yet the debate has remained unresolved and inconclusive. One reason for this has been the tendency for writers to view the Giant either in a purely local context or in a purely general historical or mythological context. A dimension that has been missed altogether is the palaeo-geographical approach. It is necessary to view the site as it has undergone economic, political and religious changes through history, but always within a geographical perspective.

Landscape studies have reached a stage now where we can reconstruct the ancient landscapes of the South Downs at various periods of history with some degree of confidence. Some elements in the landscape remain surprisingly constant over long periods: for example, the altitudes of the chalk hill tops and the position of the imposing escarpment. Other elements have changed significantly, such as the changes in sea level that are discussed in Chapter 10 and that produced some startling results.

It was, I suppose, inevitable that, as a geographer, I should sense the importance of the geographical setting in the resolution of the Wilmington mystery. Without that sense, the significance of the relationships among certain sites would be lost. Without it, one could not perceive why certain places should have been regarded as special, or even unique, by cultures that were often much more sensitive to landscape than our own.

A sympathy for the downland landscape of the present day is an essential starting-point for a study such as this. My own feelings for the chalk hills are not unlike those expressed by Gilbert White in the quotation that opened this chapter. I may not agree with his somewhat fanciful explanation of the quality of the landscape; I nevertheless share his enthusiasm for the hills and his sense that a kind of organic dynamism is at work beneath the thin green skin of the Downs. W. H. Hudson convincingly described the peculiar kind of excitement which the hills create, in *Nature in Downland* (1942).

Here are no inviting woods and mysterious green shades that ask to be explored: they stand naked to the sky, and on them the mind becomes more aerial, less conscious of gravity and a too solid body . . . It is true that the extent of earth visible from the very highest downs is not really great, but with a succession of dome-like outlines extending to the horizon we have to take into account the illusion of infinite distance produced on the mind by the repetition of similar forms. The architect, in a small way, produces the same effect in his colonnades . . . Once we have got above the world, and have an unobstructed view all round, whether the height above the surrounding country be 500 or 5,000 feet, then we at once experience all that sense of freedom, triumph and elation which the mind is capable of.

It is among these modestly proportioned yet majestic hills that the great, silent figure of the Giant patiently awaits the solution of the mystery of his origin. Known variously as the Wilmington Giant or the Long Man of Wilmington, he stands on a hillside four miles north-west of Eastbourne, some two hundred and forty feet tall in his original state. If — strange fancy — he were able to tear himself from his turf prison, rise up from the hills and stride to Canterbury, he would by several feet overtop Bell Harry, the central tower of the Cathedral.

So perfectly proportioned are the hills and so well are the Giant's limbs accommodated on the hillside that the absolute immensity of his size does not at first register. He is obviously colossal, but it comes as something of a surprise to discover that he is the largest representation of the human form in the eastern hemisphere. In view of its exceptional character, it is difficult to account for the lack of sustained and committed interest in the figure. Many thousands of visitors come to look at the Long Man every year, with a curiosity that deserves to be satisfied. There are many reasons for the lack of intensive research; the totality of the mystery surrounding the Giant and the lack of even a provisional identification go part of the way towards explaining it. The Giant is too anonymous: it is too completely lacking in history, identity, cultural associations. It is ultimately too inscrutable to capture the popular imagination and retain the interest of the public at large. The Statue of Liberty, which is only two-thirds as tall as the Giant, is known with affection the world over, principally because it is clearly identified with an idea that is well understood.

It is hoped that this book may go some way towards restoring the balance. The mystery of the Wilmington Giant's identity has at last been unravelled. When all the evidence is sifted and carefully considered, the figure emerges as a portrait of truly colossal importance. Now that its identity, age, provenance and purpose are established, the Giant should be restored — both historically and physically — to its rightful place among the great monuments of the ancient world.

MUSINGS ON THE LONG MAN
There has been repeated discussion of the Giant's origin and identity, but it has been of a rather short-winded and intermittent nature. There was a concerted attempt to get to the bottom of the mystery in the 1920s, when the *Herald* magazine opened its pages to a public forum on the subject. The editor, Arthur Beckett, invited anyone with a view on the Giant's origin to contribute. Theory after theory was put forward and, at the time, it was felt that the matter was thoroughly thrashed out. In fact, no conclusion was reached. Arthur Beckett opened the discussion with the idea that the Long Man was Beowulf and J. E. Ray followed with the theory that he was a Saxon haymaker. Hadrian Allcroft, always to the fore in any discussion of the antiquities of Sussex, came out with the rather surprising view that the figure was made relatively recently. Others suggested that the Giant was Wotan or Baldur or a sidereal clock.

It was Arthur Beckett who had earlier written one of the most sensitive and authentic travelogue books about the South Downs. His *Spirit of the Downs*, which was published in 1909, is, I think, the earliest as well as one of the finest pieces in the genre, full of solid, well-informed and well-observed detail. Beckett's great sympathy for the downland scene comes out well in the chapter on the Long Man, 'The Hero on the Hill'. He describes how he lay down in the right foot of the Long Man and mused on the possible origins of the great figure.

I thought of the theory of the Benedictine Monks of Wilmington Priory: that they had cut this gigantic figure on the turf as a pastime . . . I thought also of that theological theory which suggests the image that fell down from Jupiter, as recorded in the Acts of the Apostles . . . I thought of the Colossus of Rhodes, representing Helios, which wonder was of half the proportions of the Giant of Wilmington; also of the image set up by Nebuchadnezzar, and those of the Assyrian sculptors; of the smaller Chryselephantine statue of Athena on the Acropolis; of Zeus at Olympia and Tarentum; of the bronze Apollo of Apollonia and the famous marble Nero. But thinking of these enormous images gave me no clue to the origin of the more enormous Long Man of Wilmington . . . Arousing myself from these speculations I turned to look at the landscape. Over Mount Caburn lay Lewes and, leftward, Firle Beacon, with an outline like a human arm placed akimbo. Distances were lost in liquid blue, and from the blue above a lark showered its song on the world of the Downs. Dark woods gleamed in a sudden glare of the sun. The grey scar of an old chalk-pit lay on my left. Behind me was the lonely Long Man asking the traveller — like the Sphinx — to solve the dark mystery of its own origin.

The sphinx-like Giant, perplexed about his own beginnings, continued to pose the same mute questions to his visitors long after Arthur Beckett's Edwardian meditation. The press debate that Beckett led from July 1923 until January 1924 did not produce the answers. It did, however, assemble a range of possibilities and a certain amount of evidence. These were taken up again fifteen years later by J. B. Sidgwick, who wrote a review of both evidence and theories. Well balanced and unbiased though his discussion was, Sidgwick was able to reach no conclusion at all, but he did provoke another burst of public interest in the Long Man. Sidgwick's article was quickly followed by another specifically advocating a Roman origin for the Long Man (Heron-Allen, 1939), and by letters offering various scraps of evidence and counter-evidence. The Editor of the *Sussex County Magazine* commented that Volume 13 of the journal had been 'busy' with ideas on the Long Man.

One intention in writing a book on the Long Man is to re-open that discussion and, I hope, inform it with much more detailed and up-to-date evidence than was sought or indeed was available in the 1920s and 1930s. Curiously, the idea of writing this book came to me in much the same way that Arthur Beckett's extraordinary Saxon battle fantasy (omitted from the earlier quotation) came to him; in other words while actually lying on the shape of the Giant. Beckett lay on the Giant's right foot; I lay on the Giant's forehead. Whether the new location was any more effective is for the reader to judge.

The form of the book came to me as suddenly and in the same place. The Giant has gone through many transformations in the minds of men, so the most natural way of approaching the problem of his true identity is by way of the historical transformations through which he has passed. Indeed, he has passed through so many different guises in the various theories put forward in the last century alone that the outline is analogous to a primal theme or *leitmotiv* in music, a raw and concentrated cipher susceptible of endless variation and development.

The psychological equivalent of the musical *leitmotiv* is the archetype. The archetype is a primordial and archaic image residing in the unconscious mind: an image that symbolizes an idea, a form or a force which is fundamental to the human spirit (Jung, 1956). The powerful images contained in the collective myths, or even in great individual works of art, are often external expressions of archetypes. The way in which the Long Man fires so many images of gods or heroes is a sure indication that it too is an expression of some powerful archetype.

When I began my own personal quest for the Giant's identity, I had no idea where it would lead me. I started out with neither preference nor bias but exposed my outer mind to the conventional ratiocination of evidence and argument and my inner mind to the psychological triggers inherent in the many different interpretations. The result, which was not at all a foregone conclusion, was that the two separate activities converged on a single interpretation that satisfied on both levels. It brings the identity, the date of origin, the creators and the original purpose of the Giant into a sharper focus than I could ever have hoped for when I started out.

My purpose is to tell of bodies which have been transformed into shapes of a different kind. You heavenly powers, since you were responsible for those changes, as for all else, look favourably on my attempts, and spin an unbroken thread from the earliest beginnings of the world down to my own times.

(Ovid, *Metamorphoses*, Book I.)

2. THE GIANT DESCRIBED

Had a charming ramble with my brother, we mounted Windore Hill. I had no idea of the beautiful diversity which the hill affords; nor could I have imagined that deep snow and cold winds had such charms.

Mary Capper's Diary, February 1782.

THE SITE

Windover Hill is a hill that would conjure the splendour of majesty in our imaginations, even if there had never been kings. In sun, rain, wind or snow, the hill communicates a specialness that seems to be inherent in the form itself, a quality of being 'other than' all the surrounding landscape. Its antiquity and the nebulous, mostly prehistoric associations it has gathered to itself over several millennia have intensified this quality. As later chapters will show, its position, its stately form and the superb views from its summit and slopes have attracted physical and spiritual activity of a peculiar intensity and purposefulness.

The commanding, tranquil summit of Windover Hill is on the northern rim of the South Downs. To the north, the hill side falls away abruptly with a maximum slope of 35°, providing the site of the great drawing. The steep slope is just one short stretch of the South Downs escarpment, which runs 65 miles from Beachy Head to Old Winchester Hill — a dramatic inland cliff passing right through Sussex and into east Hampshire.

The escarpment is interrupted by four major river gaps, the

valleys of the Arun, Adur, Ouse and Cuckmere, which divide the South Downs into five separate massifs. The Giant is located on the easternmost massif, which is a small diamond of downland between the River Cuckmere and Beachy Head, the last outpost of the South Downs before the destructive waves of the Channel blot out all further traces of the chalk outcrop. The south-western and south-eastern edges of the easternmost block are still being actively eroded, as the fresh, white, vertical cliffs attest. The north-western edge is marked by the water meadows of the Cuckmere valley, and the north-eastern edge by the recently drained marshes of Pevensey Levels. Inside this naturally isolated block of hill country, only four miles square, all the rich variety of downland scenery is to be found: dense forests, careening and billowing wheatfields and, above all, the green swell of downland pasture. It offers shaded dells and coombes on the one hand and hilltops swept by wind and sun on the other.

The escarpment has been eroded by melting snows during the Ice Age to form short gullies or coombes. The many embayments and re-entrants that have resulted give the northern edge of the Downs a crenellated appearance. The Giant stands on the back wall of one of the embayments so that, when the figure is seen from due north, it has an added theatricality; but the shallow amphitheatre also obstructs the view from the north-west and north-east, so from some angles, often unexpectedly, the Giant cannot be seen. The site chosen by the mysterious creators of the Long Man is thus curiously ambivalent; it both exhibits and conceals.

The steep slope (about 28°) on which the Giant is drawn is almost a plane surface, so smooth that it has even been suggested that the hill side was specially levelled before the figure was marked out. The smooth slope has in fact been produced by the two gullies that bound the back wall of the shallow coombe. Given that the figure was originally cut out of the turf, it is hard to imagine anyone removing the turf from the entire site, lowering and smoothing the rock surface, then replacing the turf — and all this before the Giant was even marked out. It looks as if this coombe was selected from many possible escarpment amphitheatres along the Downs simply because it had the natural slope qualities required and afforded sufficient space to carry a large hill figure. But it was by no means the only possible site.

One hundred feet above the Giant's head is the crest of the South Downs escarpment, which forms a smooth skyline and was used well back into prehistory as an easy routeway across the country. A long, sloping spur rises from the Cuckmere at Alfriston, climbing gradually to the summits of Windover Hill (620 feet), Wilmington Hill (702 feet) and Folkington Hill (630 feet). To the east, the crest drops to 286 feet in the windgap of the Oxen Dean valley. Then, after another gentle climb, the escarpment rises to Combe Hill (620 feet) and stays at roughly that altitude as it curves southwards to Beachy Head via the summits of Cold Crouch, Babylon Down and Willingdon Hill.

Several of the hill summits carry archaeological remains that are relevant to a discussion of the Long Man's origins. Certainly the most important of these is Windover Hill, since it carries the image of the Long Man and is crowded with vestiges of prehistoric activity, which will be described in later chapters.

The figure has its head at an altitude of 500 feet above sea level. Since it spans an altitudinal range of 100 feet, even though resting back at an angle of 28°, under some weather conditions the upper part is eerily lost in the clouds and only the legs are visible. Normally, though, the entire figure can be seen and, had it eyes to see, it would have a commanding view across a large area of the Weald of Sussex towards the wooded skyline of St Leonard's Forest and Ashdown Forest. Crowborough Beacon, at 787 feet the loftiest point in the High Weald, is conspicuous on the horizon to the north.

THE FIGURE

The most impressive thing about the Giant himself is his size; from the tips of his toes to the crown of his head he measures 231 feet. He is standing, facing us out of the hillside with his legs spread the width of his shoulders apart. His arms are partially extended on each side and his hands, raised to shoulder level, are holding what appear to be lances, spears or staves. The design is almost symmetrical, with the two vertical staves forming two sides of an incomplete rectangular frame. The illusion of a frame has unfortunately been reinforced by the well-meant addition of protective fences round the figure. The fences only serve to obstruct people walking over the Giant and merely intensify erosion in certain places. The earlier simplicity of the figure, before the fences were added, can be appreciated from the earliest known photograph of the Giant, taken in 1874. The only significant departure from symmetry is to be found in the legs, which are both turned to the

Giant's right. The feet and calf muscles are thus depicted in profile and might lead us to interpret the figure as walking eastwards. The general mien of the figure is nevertheless one of great and powerful repose.

The figure is marked in outline only. There are no tell-tale details of dress, ornament or facial features that could help us to identify the Giant. He is naked, featureless, enigmatic. All he shows us are the 235 feet long staves and even they are hard to interpret. Are they ceremonial weapons, like Thor's hammer, to indicate the figure's rank, status or function? Do they perhaps recall an event such as a survey that involved the use of ranging rods? Or are they the leading edges of two great doors? The staves — whatever they are — give us the best opportunity we have of identifying the mysterious figure.

A further clue resides in the figure's dimensions. Each foot is as large as a family car; his legs are exactly 100 feet long and as wide as a country lane even at the knees. His waist is 23 feet wide, his hips 28 feet and his shoulders 46 feet. Each arm is 85 feet long. His neck is about 11 feet long and his head is 31 feet long and 19 feet across. From heel to crown he is 227 feet tall, which makes him only 50 feet shorter than the tower and spire of Chichester Cathedral. Other representations of the human form from other lands and other cultures are dwarfed by the Long Man. The seated pharaohs carved out of rock at Abu Simbel are described as colossal, yet *three* of these great statues, each 67 feet high, placed on top of one another would still be shorter than the Long Man.

The Giant has been drawn with enormous care and deliberation. To achieve the degree of symmetry displayed by the figure, a great deal of planning, measurement and preliminary marking out must have been involved before the turf cutting began. The symmetry is very impressive, but not perfect, as measurements between the staves and the head reveal. The distance between the head and the right stave is 50 feet 11 inches: that between the head and the left stave is 46 feet 8 inches. The staves appear to be parallel, but that feature is also slightly deceptive. The distance between the staves at the top of the figure is 116 feet 9 inches. At the foot of the figure the distance has decreased by more than two feet to 114 feet 8 inches.

One of the most fascinating aspects of the drawing is the elongation that gives the figure its name. It has been drawn long and thin deliberately, so that even though it rests on a 28° slope it is still easily recognizable when viewed from lower down the hill side.

Given the heel-to-crown height of 227 feet, the shoulder width of 46 feet and the hip width of 28 feet, the Long Man has been drawn 1.9 times the height of a well-proportioned man on the same lateral scale. Correcting for the exaggeration, the Long Man has the same proportions as a man 5 feet 10 inches tall with 27-inch shoulders and 18-inch hips; in other words, he has the build of an apparently athletic and muscular man.

If the elongation can be corrected in this way, it should be possible to calculate the viewpoint from which the carvers intended us to see the figure. In fact the proportions only appear correct from the air, about 4° up from a horizontal extending northwards from the figure. Since there is no solid vantage point along that line in the Vale of Sussex, one can only conclude that the proportions were not calculated exactly, and that a certain degree of disproportion was accepted. It means that the Giant was always seen, at least from in front and by earthbound man, as a broad and stocky figure who had, to all appearances, the build of a short man.

EARTH FIGURES IN THE NEW WORLD
Before attempting to set the Wilmington Giant in his local, English context, it is worth digressing briefly to look at earth figures in the Americas; for it is apparent that monuments to the nobility of the human form, or to concepts symbolized by it, have been made by many peoples widely separated in space and time. To look at the American earth drawings, or geoglyphs as they are sometimes called, is not in any way to imply contact among the makers of such works. There is no suggestion, for example, that all large geoglyphs are the product of a single culture.

One group of earth drawings that is comparatively little known in Europe is to be found on the flat river terraces of the Colorado near Blythe in California. The drawings were first noticed by geologist W. P. Blake in 1854, when he was prospecting for a railway route to the Pacific coast; but they only attracted public and scientific attention when air photographs became available in the 1930s. Of the three groups of figures at Blythe, the first comprises a spiral, a quadruped and a giantess 91 feet tall; the second, half a mile away, consists of a quadruped and a giantess 168 feet high; the third consists of a single, isolated giant 105 feet high with stones to represent the genital organs. Across the border, at Sacaton in Arizona, is a fourth group: this time a 175 feet high giant or giantess is accompanied by a smaller, child-like figure. The Pime

Indians call the Sacaton Giant Ha'ak Va'ak, meaning 'Ha'ak lying down'. Ha'ak was a mythical child-eating ogress who was eventually killed by an Indian hero called Elder Brother. It is thought that all these figures are relatively modern, dating from between 1550 and 1850, and may all depict events in the Ha'ak saga.

In South America are the much more famous Nazca figures. Although more sophisticated and geometrical in design, the Nazca drawings were made in much the same way as the Blythe and Sacaton figures. The loose material on the flat desert surface, darkened and 'varnished' by weathering, has been dug or swept to one side to reveal the pale, unpatinated layer beneath. The Nazca figures are large, stylized drawings of a wide variety of organic forms, including birds, lizards, spiders, monkeys and flowers, ranging in size from about 100 feet up to 620 feet.

It may be significant that these pictures of relatively humble organisms are drawn on the level surfaces of the desert, whilst the more commanding hillsides are reserved for images of the human form. The largest of the human figures, and indeed the largest of all the giants, is the Giant of Atacama. His image is drawn on the side of an isolated mountain, Sierra Unica, in northern Chile. Drawn against a frieze of smaller, less distinct figures, the Giant of Atacama stands an impressive 393 feet high. He wears boots and a crown and his symmetrical, frontal pose is similar to that of the Wilmington Giant, though without the staves. Only the head gives pause for thought; it is almost panther-like and may represent an animal mask. If indeed it is intended to be a man, this awe-inspiring geoglyph is the largest representation of a human form in the world. It is thought to date, along with the other Atacama drawings, from around two thousand years ago. If the colossal size of the Giant of Atacama seems to dwarf the Long Man, it should be remembered that the Giant at Wilmington is still the second largest in the world, after the desert giant and his band of Inca warriors (Gerster, 1976).

HILL FIGURES IN ENGLAND

The earth drawings scattered across 850 miles of the Atacama Desert are thought to have been produced by a single culture, the Inca. Is it possible that, within a much smaller area, the hill figures of England also belong to a single culture? The natural next step is an examination of the other English hill figures, to see whether any common purpose, style, date or culture can be detected.

The chalk hills in particular lend themselves to the creation of hill figures. The chalk soils are thin and therefore easily cut away to expose the bedrock; chalk is white and so shows up well against the living turf; hill slopes up to 35° tilt the figures so that they can be seen clearly from far away. It should be no surprise, therefore, to find that the two best known hill figures, the Cerne Giant and the Uffington White Horse, are marked out on chalk hill sides.

The Giant at Cerne Abbas in Dorset is possibly the most important for our purposes, since it is a representation of a human form, male, colossal: he is apparently a relation of the Long Man of Wilmington. At 180 feet, the Cerne Giant is significantly shorter than the Long Man. The dimensions of most of his limbs are proportionally smaller as well; the legs, for example, are only 80 feet long, compared with the Long Man's 100 feet, and the head is 22 feet long, compared with the Long Man's 31 feet. The Cerne Giant's right arm, at 109 feet, is significantly longer than the Long Man's, and he is using this exaggerated limb to brandish an enormous knobbed club 121 feet long, which is held menacingly and diagonally above his head.

In the eighteenth century, some letters were visible between his feet. The Revd de St Croix, writing a hundred years ago, recorded that in 1772 there were three letters surmounted by three numbers. They have all long since vanished, which is surprising since the rest of the figure has been meticulously preserved by local villagers. On some air photographs, the irregular ground between the feet seems still to hold traces of the mysterious lettering. The letters seem to be 'CLID'. Walter of Coventry, writing in the thirteenth century, said that the Cerne Giant was called Helith, so perhaps the 'rude inscription' is really an early form of the Giant's name, with the apparent 'C' intended as an 'E'. The soft *th* sound for 'D' suggests a Celtic origin. We will return to the possible origins and interpretations of the Cerne Giant later: for the moment, his morphology is our main concern.

The Cerne Giant is similar to the Wilmington Giant in that he faces us, naked, with his arms partially extended and his legs turned in profile to the right. But there the similarities end. The right arm is upraised with a club. The left is extended and holds nothing, though it appears likely that it once held a sword, dagger, spear or staff. More startling are the extra details shown within the outline of the figure. The hands are divided up so that fingers and thumbs are visible. The face is marked with mouth, eyes and eye-brows. The body has nipples, ribs and even a penis and testicles. In addition, the figure is wearing a belt or thong round the waist. The Long Man has none of these details, only the outline, yet there can be no doubting that the Long Man too is masculine.

There is one more significant difference between the two giants. The Cerne Giant, with his erect phallus, a prodigious 29 feet long, and his huge knobbed club, is altogether a more unruly and antic figure than the Long Man. The Cerne Giant seems to be a fertility god on the rampage. The Wilmington Giant, by contrast, is commanding, dignified and majestic.

Two more figures rest under the grass on Plymouth Hoe. Since the figures themselves are lost, we have to depend on folk tradition for descriptions of them. Such notoriously fragile evidence has to be treated with due caution. It is alleged that the two figures represented Corineus and Gogmagog. Corineus was a Trojan leader who was supposed, in English folklore, to have come to Britain with Brutus. Corineus and his men decided to settle in Cornwall, where most of the giants, the native inhabitants of Britain, had taken refuge. The Trojan party was attacked by the giants, led by Gogmagog, who was a lout 12 feet tall and strong enough to uproot oak trees. In the ensuing battle, all the giants were killed except Gogmagog. Corineus took him on single-handed and, after wrestling with the giant for a while, managed to hurl him into the sea. It is just possible that this depiction of victor and vanquished and the progressive garbling characteristic of British folklore led to the eventual division of Gogmagog into two separate giants, Gog and Magog.

A long-standing tradition of 'giants in the Hills' led T. C. Lethbridge to explore the slopes of Wandlebury Camp in the Gogmagog Hills near Cambridge. By painstakingly measuring soil depth, Lethbridge was able to map the outlines of another lost hill figure. In fact he found the highly stylized outlines of what seem to be four figures in a tableau. Lethbridge identified a man wielding a sword as Wandil, a female figure as Magog or Epona, a second male figure as Gog or the sun god, a beaked horse and a chariot. He even ventured dates for the group; Epona with her horse and chariot were cut in about 200 BC and the other figures added 150 years later. Reception of Lethbridge's work has always been guarded, and many scholars regard him as a crank. Photographs taken of the site while excavation was in progress are very difficult to interpret, even with the aid of Lethbridge's explanations. The survey method is also rather suspect, since soil depth may not be diagnostic. As we shall see, the Long Man's outlines are extremely shallow and would have been missed altogether by the Lethbridge method. Conversely, isolated deep soil profiles may be related to joint fissures in the chalk rather than to excavation in antiquity.

The stylized, exploded figures Lethbridge saw on Wandlebury Hill bear more than a passing resemblance to the broken outline of the White Horse of Uffington. This is the most immediately striking and probably the best known of all the English hill figures. Its broad white body and sweeping calligraphic lines show up across wide areas of the Vale of the White Horse. It is very large, with an overall length of 360 feet and a maximum height of 130 feet. The solid, brilliant white form of the horse is scoured every seven years to clear away any grass that may have begun to colonize the figure. The scouring used to be accompanied by a festival known as the 'pastime', which was held inside the eight-acre enclosure on the hill crest, above the figure and to its left. The fun and games were stopped in 1857, but the serious business of the seven-year scouring continued. The horse is thought to be Iron Age in origin, dedicated to the Celtic horse goddess Epona; it has been suggested that the rectangular Iron Age enclosure above the figure might have been intended as a shrine to Epona.

The Uffington White Horse is certainly ancient. It was mentioned in an ecclesiastical document at Abingdon in AD 1084; but the putative date of 100 BC would be hard to prove. There is the supporting line of evidence that similar exploded drawings of horses appear on some Celtic coins, such as the Gallic stater dated 57 BC now in the Ashmolean Museum, Oxford. On the other hand, even the identification of the figure as a horse is questionable. It has an unduly long body and very short legs. As a literal representation of a quadruped it comes closer to a dachshund. The head is also peculiar: it appears to have a beak. There is the strong possibility that the figure is a dragon, not a horse, and that the association with Epona is incorrect. One curious link with the Wilmington and Cerne Giants is the juxtaposition of hill figure and earthwork. Immediately above and to the left of each hill figure is a significant earthwork. At Uffington and Cerne Abbas it is a rectangular banked enclosure; at Wilmington it is a long barrow.

Another chalk horse is to be found further along the same escarpment, on Bratton Down in Wiltshire. This one, the Westbury White Horse, is 176 feet long and 113 feet high, dominating the Vale of Pewsey from the northern rim of Salisbury Plain. The

Westbury figure is very recognizably a horse, so perfect are its proportions, but also very recognizably a modern work. In fact it was cut in 1778. Our interest in the figure might stop there, except that a horse is known to have existed on the hillside before 1778. The 're-cutting' was unfortunately a total replacement of the original figure, which was beaked and short-legged — indeed, it sounds remarkably like the dragon-horse at Uffington. It, too, has an important earthwork in the near vicinity, in this case the ramparts of Bratton Castle, an Iron Age hilltop enclosure.

Closer to the Long Man, only 2½ miles away to the south-west, is the Hindover or Litlington White Horse. This little-known and rather overgrown figure was cut in 1924 to replace an earlier effort of 1838. It is perched at the top of a steep slope forming the west side of the Cuckmere valley. The place is called Hindover or High-and-Over and is really an ancient, grassed-over river cliff. The 300 feet high, steeply raked hillside would make an excellent site for a major hill figure and there is a local rumour — it can be rated no higher than that — to the effect that this slope once had its own giant. Who it was or what it looked like have been long forgotten.

Thirteen miles north-west of the Long Man is Plumpton Plain. In spite of its name it is a section of the South Downs escarpment rising to over 700 feet. Its steep north-facing slope once carried a great cross, but it has been allowed to grow over and can no longer be seen. It is believed locally that the cross was cut in the Middle Ages to commemorate those who died at the Battle of Lewes in 1264. This may be so, but the north-facing slope of Mount Harry, where the battle took place, would seem a better choice of site. Since Plumpton Plain is 1½ miles to the west, it looks suspiciously as though a chalk mark of some kind was already cut into the hillside there and that it was taken over and possibly adapted to make it commemorate the great battle.

Similar marks are known from Buckinghamshire and Oxfordshire. The Whiteleaf Cross on the Chilterns escarpment at Princes Risborough may have started off as some kind of magical or zodiacal cipher and later redesigned in the Christian era to make it into a cross. The White Mark at Watlington in Oxfordshire, seven miles to the south-west, has evidently not been adapted, since it looks like nothing recognizable.

Of the many frivolous modern hill figures, such as zoo animals, or regimental insignia, or the paltry coronation 'ER' at Lewes, or the equestrian George III riding, cured but comical, away from his Weymouth bathing holiday, nothing more need be said. It is only the ancient and serious figures that are of interest in the quest for the Long Man's origins, since it is evident that the Long Man is himself both ancient and serious.

Of the lost and apocryphal figures, it is hard to decide how many to include. There are tantalizing glimpses of yet another giant who is supposed to have embellished the Corallian Limestone slopes of Shotover Hill, east of Oxford. The Red Horse of Tysoe in Warwickshire was also overgrown and lost, but rediscovered in the 1960s by Miller and Carrdus. Nearby, S. G. Wildman believes that he found a whole tableau of figures. The shadowy forms are interpreted as a human form waving a whip, a goose with its head pointing up in the air and an unidentified beast which might be a horse, a lion or a dragon. Beneath this remarkable frieze, and running the full length of the tableau, Wildman saw a poorly defined fifth creature which was impossible to identify. Wildman believes that the postulated human form represents the Saxon god Tiw, after whom Tysoe was named, and that the myth depicted may be the binding of an evil beast or the succession of the seasons; but it is all very uncertain.

Hill figures in general are difficult to interpret. There are disagreements concerning dates, cultural origins, identities and even, in some cases, the existence of the figures. It is clear that an element of subjectivity is involved in interpreting 'lost' figures such as the Wandlebury and Tysoe groups. But it will also emerge in later chapters of this book that even clearly marked figures like the Wilmington Giant and the Cerne Giant can be interpreted in a variety of ways. As far as the Wilmington Giant is concerned, a double problem presents itself. On the surface, the figure of the Giant stands revealed: he shows the onlooker his wands of office and seems as if he is waiting to be recognized and invoked by name. But there is a second figure on Windover Hill — a buried giant.

THE GIANT REVEALED, 1874-1980

The last phase in the Wilmington Giant's history began in 1874. The Duke of Devonshire, who owned the site, handed it over to the Sussex Archaeological Trust for restoration. The figure was then marked out with yellow bricks by the Revd de St Croix and a team of helpers. It is often a slight disappointment to visitors when they discover that the pallid grey lines they have seen from a distance are not, after all, the living chalk. It is to be hoped that one day the figure will be fully restored down to bedrock. It would be a much more striking and imposing monument if its outline were cut right through the turf and soil to a one-foot wide strip of white chalk. More important still, it would be a more authentic monument.

The Revd de St Croix, whose academic interest in the Giant is undisputed, bricked the figure in as an early piece of rescue archaeology. The urban rescue digs of the present day are familiar enough. As a site is cleared for development, the archaeologists

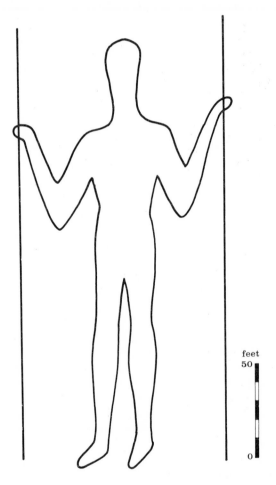

feet
50

0

Figure 1. The Wilmington Giant. The figure as marked out by the Revd de St Croix in 1874 — and as it is seen today.

retrieve what they can before the subsoil and rock are torn out to build foundations for a new building. In 1870, the Wilmington Giant was in danger for a different reason. For as long as anyone could remember, the Giant had been grassed over. The outline was marked by shallow depressions in the turf and these could only be seen when the light slanted low across the figure, especially in early morning and late evening.

The outline had always been elusive, but by 1870 it was becoming so faint that it would soon be gone completely. The lower half of the figure was particularly difficult to discern. This may be explained by the phenomenon of solifluxion or soil creep. Helped by frost, rainwash and gravity, individual particles of soil tend to migrate slowly down a slope, and there is a natural tendency for the soil on the lower part of the slope to become thicker. Thus it was that the Giant's legs began to disappear.

The Sussex Archaeological Trust decided to mark the whole outline straight away, before the Giant vanished. To this end, 7,000 yellow bricks were pulled up to the Giant in a trolley powered by a second trolley running down the hillside and weighted with children. The bricking of the Giant did not meet with universal approval even at the time it was carried out. Several criticisms were voiced in the local press, but the main objection was to the Giant's feet. It was said that the left foot had been twisted to point to the east, whereas it had originally pointed to the west. We must remember that the feet were the most indistinct parts of the figure before the bricking. In 1874, the Revd T. Bunston was vicar of Arlington, the next parish to Wilmington and, like Wilmington, overseen by the Giant. His experience, in a not very busy parish, was of viewing the Giant under many different lights and he was certain that the feet originally faced the observer. Another contemporary inhabitant remembered that the turf Giant appeared to be standing on tiptoe. One of the most interesting and reliable witnesses of the Giant's condition before 1874 was Mrs Ann Downs.

Mrs Downs lived in Wilmington Priory from about 1850 to about 1860, before moving to Seaford. She had a ringside seat at the Priory from which she could clearly see the subtleties of the Giant's outline under an infinite variety of lighting and atmospheric conditions. Mrs Downs was fascinated by the Giant. Day after day, she used to look across to the secretive coombe where the Giant lay hidden under his blankets of soil and grass, watching as he appeared and disappeared in the changing light. She felt that the Giant was a secret being who was to be seen only at certain times. The dusky slanting lights of sunrise and sunset were the right times; it was then that she was intended to see him.

So, for Ann Downs, the whole idea of the bricking was crass and insensitive. But she was sure — and this is more important for us — that the feet were restored wrongly. Her interest in the Giant and her contemplative daily viewing of the figure over a period of a decade must weigh heavily in any assessment of her opinion on this point of fact. The feet, she insisted, should be splayed and pointing down the hillside. The Giant was not walking to Eastbourne but coming down the hill.

Ann Downs' memory of the splayed, downward-pointing feet is given independent support by a rare and recently-discovered photograph, a copy of which now resides in the Barbican Museum in Lewes. It shows the Long Man immediately after the bricking, probably in April 1874, the date when the *Eastbourne Gazette* announced that G. & R. Lavis, a local photographic firm, had just issued a set of three views of the figure. The one surviving photograph shows the whitewashed brick outline very clearly. The crisp white outline of the Giant's left leg overlaps a faint image in the turf of an alternative position for the entire left leg, not just the left foot.

The turf image proves the dissenters right. The Giant's left foot *did* originally point to the west, not to the east. It *did* originally point down the slope, as if the Giant was coming down the hillside or standing on tiptoe. So, we are left wondering why the position of the leg was altered. To begin with, we must remember that the photograph was taken under conditions that favoured the revelation of such a feature. It is evident from the shadows of two horses in the picture that the photograph was taken one sunny spring afternoon, with a clear, slanting light. We must also remember that the depressions marking the leg were so slight that they could easily have been overlooked by men walking about on the figure. The restoration team was uncertain about the form of the lower legs. The assumption was made that both feet were turned to the Giant's right, for the rather naive reason that the Cerne Giant's feet were turned in that way. Even so, it is remarkable that the restorers, who must surely have seen the photograph that shows the results of their labours so well, either did not notice the correct outline of the left leg in the turf or, if they did, chose not to rectify their mistake.

What is needed is an excavation of the entire site, including the

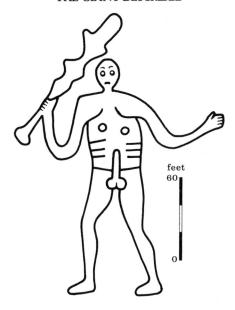

feet
60

0

Figure 2. The Cerne Giant. A hundred and eighty feet high, the giant at Cerne Abbas in Dorset is only three-quarters the size of the Wilmington Giant.

areas beyond the staves, to check that the surface outline corresponds with the cut figure at the soil-bedrock interface and that no details have been lost. When the 1874 bricks were replaced recently, four trial trenches were dug, crossing the head, right shoulder, right stave and right leg. The bricks rest in the thin topsoil, about four inches deep, and below this is a layer of chalky subsoil up to eighteen inches deep, resting on the solid chalk. The bedrock was found to be hollowed slightly below the brick outline in each case except the shoulder, where the natural slope of the rock surface was uninterrupted. The other three trenches showed that the original outline was about one foot across, except along the stave which seems to have been 2 feet 6 inches across. The depressions in the bedrock are only two inches deep, which is extremely shallow by comparison with the trenches marking the Cerne Giant and Uffington White Horse. The shallowness of the chalk figure indicates that the Wilmington Giant was created as a conventional chalk hill figure, that it was kept scoured for a period of time and that after relatively few scourings it was abandoned.

The brick outline of 1874 was repainted, usually every three years, to simulate the white chalk beneath. This practice only lapsed during the Second World War, when the Giant was painted green in order to foil enemy navigators who might otherwise have used him as a landmark. In 1946 the green giant was painted white again. Meanwhile, the figure had been gradually deteriorating due

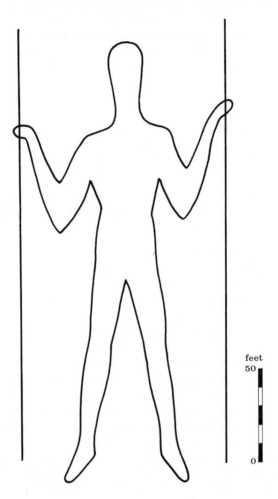

feet
50

0

Figure 3. The reconstructed Giant. The figure's legs are corrected to their pre-1874 positions. The reconstruction is based on the Phené drawing and photographic evidence.

to weathering and vandalism. By the 1960s, many of the bricks were disintegrating or missing, so the Sussex Archaeological Trust decided to replace them. This time the figure was marked in larger, pre-cast concrete blocks, which were made with white cement so that they would not need painting. B. V. Walker and Son of the nearby village of Selmeston supervised the installation of the two-foot long kerb stones, manufactured at Uckfield by C. T. Concrete Mouldings Ltd. Walkers used two tractors to winch the blocks up to the Long Man on a trolley improvised from a milk float, a bedstead and a stable door. The concrete Giant, which was finished in 1969, is composed of 770 grey kerb stones. At a cost of £800, the Wilmington Giant must still rank as one of the cheapest, as well as one of the most enigmatic, of England's national monuments.

THE TURF GIANT, 1766-1874

Descriptions and drawings of the Giant before his 'posthumous' career as a brick figure or concrete figure are tantalizingly rare. There is, of course, the useful description by Ann Downs, who knew the turf figure well. It is unfortunate that we are dependent on hearsay in the period before the bricking; no photographs have yet come to light.

There are, nevertheless, three nineteenth-century sketches drawn before the restoration. The Revd W. C. Plenderleath gathered material for his book *The White Horses of the West of England* a long time prior to publication in 1892. He drew an undated sketch of the Long Man which shows the feet missing; the lowest third of each stave is missing too. Other drawings were made by J. S. Phené, who lectured on the Long Man in London in May 1873 and displayed some of his sketches during his lecture. The eventual fate of these drawings is not known, but a copy of one of them was reproduced in *The Graphic* on 7 February 1874. The figure appears very similar to that shown in the Plenderleath drawing, with both staves and legs petering out towards the lower edge of the image. The third, and probably the oldest, of the nineteenth-century drawings is the anonymous sketch appearing in the *Sussex Archaeological Collection*, Volume 4, which is specifically dated 1850. It shows the left-hand stave stopping short just below the Giant's knee, the right-hand stave almost complete and the feet missing. The only significant difference between this and the later drawings is that the face is shown as a closed circle or, in other words, with a chin.

Figure 4. The Phené drawing. The Wilmington Giant was sketched by Dr Phené immediately before the restoration undertaken in the spring of 1874.

Horsfield, in his *History of Sussex* (1835), gives a short description of the Giant as a figure detectable by differences in the verdure. The Giant was then evidently in the same state as it was twenty years later, when Ann Downs saw it. Horsfield mentions the staves and gives the figure's height as 240 feet. This may seem too high a figure but, when the dimensions of the restored brick outline are taken, and then allowance made for the extension of the original left toe *below* the modern outline, the full height of the turf Giant would be 239 or 240 feet. It is clear that Horsfield or his source actually went over the Giant with a tape measure.

In Gough's edition of Camden's *Britannia* (1806) there is no evidence of personal acquaintance with the figure. Gough gives the height of the Giant as 140 feet, which is intolerably inaccurate. He does, however, add some information about the mysterious staves. One is said to be a rake, the other a scythe. These details are not mentioned by Horsfield and therefore were not plainly visible in 1835. They seem to derive from a curious eighteenth-century drawing, which is the earliest known representation of, or indeed reference to, the Long Man.

On both counts this drawing is of great interest. It is part of a motley collection of notes and drawings known as the Burrell

Manuscripts and which have been deposited in the British Museum. The Burrell drawing of the Long Man, dating from not later than 1766, shows the two staves as rake and scythe plainly enough, but it is hard to visualize the eight teeth shown on the rake being decipherable on a turf figure whose largest features were to be misread a hundred years later. When we come to the face and throat, suspicion mounts that this is a work of gentlemanly fancy. Not only are there eyes, but pupils; not only a chin, but locks of hair and a collar. The shading on the waist and knees was presumably put in to give an illusion of solidity to the drawing and could not conceivably have been detectable on the hillside. As if that were not enough, Sir William Burrell has added a note underneath the drawing declaring that the figure was 80 feet high.

The detail that could have been so telling, so invaluable in our search for the identity of the Giant, is hopelessly unreliable. The broad form of the figure is presumably what Sir William really saw on the northern slope of Windover Hill: a stocky, symmetrical, spreadeagled male figure, facing us out of the hillside, with his feet splayed and a stave planted vertically in each outstretched hand. The drawing tells us, at least, that the Giant existed in 1766 and

Figure 5. The Burrell drawing. Sir William Burrell made this sketch of the Giant during a visit to the area in 1766.

that it had broadly the same character as the restored figure —
apart, of course, from the alteration to the left leg.

THE GIANT BEFORE 1766

Delving into the Giant's past as far back as 1766, we find ourselves
confronted by the unsatisfactory, capering Haymaker doodled by
Sir William Burrell. Before Sir William's time, the mystery
deepens still further, for there is no known reference to the Long
Man earlier than 1766. There are three ways of interpreting the
deep silence. First, the figure could be an eighteenth-century
fabrication, in which case no earlier reference could be expected.
Second, the figure was grassed over and therefore remained unnoticed by the casual traveller and possibly by the local village folk
as well. Third, there may after all be documentary records as yet
unresearched or art works as yet unrecognized that contain references to the Long Man.

There is a superficial case for a late cutting, say, in the mid-
eighteenth century. Certainly there was a good deal of interest in
hill figures at that time. It is known, for example, that the second
Westbury Horse was cut in 1778. If the figure of the Long Man had
been recently cut when Sir William visited Wilmington, it might
explain why he saw details that had disappeared by 1835. So there
is a possibility that the figure is an eighteenth-century conceit. On
the other hand, there is incontrovertible archaeological evidence,
which will be discussed in Chapters 4 and 5, that it is much older.

On common sense grounds, it seems likely that the sheer
physical obscurity of the turf figure meant that it went unnoticed. If
the antiquity of the figure is conceded on the strength of the
archaeological evidence, and the Long Man was there on Windover
Hill during the Middle Ages, why is there virtually no surviving
folklore about him? Folklore is not usually lost lock, stock and
barrel. It is more likely that the people of Wilmington and the
neighbouring villages took little or no notice of him and that people
living outside the area did not even know that he was there. After
all, the Revd G. M. Cooper, looking at the turf figure in 1850,
wrote that 'the outline is so slightly indented in the turf that to a
close inspection it is imperceptible; but when viewed from a
distance with a strong side light, it may be plainly seen; and yet,
even then, an unpractised eye will have difficulty in tracing out the
figure, of which the lower parts are at all times extremely
indistinct'.

The third possibility, that evidence of his earlier existence survives in documents or local art work, is difficult to test. The documents in question cannot be searched for, because we have no way of knowing where or even what they may be. As for represent-ations of the Long Man in sculpture, paintings or stained glass, the search is fairly easy. All the medieval churches in the area may be visited and any possible references to the image of the Long Man recorded. In fact there are only two, and both are doubtful.

In the parish church of St Andrew, Jevington, there is a fine Saxon mural tablet of the resurrected Christ overpowering the forces of evil. It has some features in common with the Long Man. The figure is depicted frontally and the right hand is raised to hold a vertical lance. There are nevertheless more differences than similarities. The feet are together, not spread apart, and the left hand is resting on the left hip. The lance is decorated with a cross at the top and the head has a halo. In Buncton church, a Norman capital suporting the chancel arch has a small figure carved on it. The little man holds no staves; instead his hands rest on the front of his thighs. The spread legs are reminiscent of the original pre-1874 figure of the Giant, even to the diagonally downward-pointing feet. The Buncton man is surrounded by curious circular devices which may be sun symbols. But, unless there is evidence that the Wilmington Giant has to do with sun worship, there is little to connect the two images.

Considering the enormous size of the Giant, it seems strange that there are no representations of him in the surrounding villages. This is one of the many puzzles surrounding the Wilmington Giant; yet there are far greater mysteries than this and we must now address ourselves to them. The fundamental questions are the ones that occur naturally in the minds of most visitors to the Giant. The first sight of the Giant is, for some reason, always a sudden experience and it always excites the same questions. Who is it? Who made him? When? Why?

Many theories have been floated to attempt answers to one or more of these questions and each one must be considered on its own merits before we can draw any conclusion. We must review *all* the possibilities. Who is the buried Giant? Is he man or god? Who cut his colossal portrait in the hillside? When was the image made? Why was it put there: for fun, fear or faith? Why was the Giant abandoned? Each question breeds ten more questions, and the answers are elusive. We will need to keep all our wits about us as we enter the spiral maze.

3. THE QUEST

And questing after it, my spirit sought to comprehend the splendour it had seen, but found it not as a creature and could not get away from created things, that it might embrace that uncreated and uncomprehended splendour. Nevertheless it wandered everywhere and strove to behold it. It searched through the air, it wandered over the heavens, it crossed the abysses; it searched, so it seemed, to the ends of the world. But in all that it found nothing, for all was created. And I lamented and was sorrowful and my heart burned, and I lived as one distraught in mind. But it came as it was wont and, descending as a luminous cloud, seemed to envelop my whole head, so that I cried dismayed. But, flying away again, it left me alone. I realized suddenly that it was within me, and in the midst of my heart it shone like the light of a spherical sun.

Symeon, the 'New Theologian' (AD 970-1040), *Love Songs to God*.

After at least a century of speculation, a number of theories, insights and intuitions have emerged on the Long Man of Wilmington that are well worth discussing in detail. One of the most disappointing aspects of the extensive yet short-winded literature on the Long Man is that each theory has been launched on a saucer of factual and circumstantial evidence; so little, in fact, that it has been impossible to judge whether the theory floats, let alone whether it will withstand the heavy seas of argument and counter-evidence. It is the aim of this review to treat the many versions of the Giant's origins discursively, so that we can pursue as many as possible of the lines of evidence that have been, or might be, offered by both supporters and opponents of the different theories.

We have plenty of evidence for the Giant's existence in the nineteenth century and one manuscript that proves his existence in the mid-eighteenth century. It seems natural, in the quest for the Long Man's origins, that we should carefully leaf back through history, reversing time itself.

One popular view is that the figure originated in the Middle Ages as the work of monks from Wilmington Priory, and various motives have been suggested or implied. The monks may have been heretical and set up the Giant as an idol during a genuine reversion to pre-Christian beliefs. Alternatively, it may have been offered as a cynical concession to irresistible pressure from parishioners who still owed some loyalty to the Old Religion. A third possibility is that the monks subscribed to a secret, kabbalistic version of Christianity, not unlike that of the Templars. A fourth is that the Giant was carved to represent a conventional biblical figure or a pilgrim; in other words, the monks were not heretics. A fifth view is the one suggested by Horsfield in 1835: that the monks cut the figure for no good reason, either for fun or out of sheer boredom with life at the Priory.

WILMINGTON PRIORY AND THE MEDIEVAL MONKS
Wilmington Priory stands at the southern end of Wilmington village, with only a cluster of later farm buildings between it and the Long Man. What survives is mainly a restoration of the medieval structure. Neither the thirteenth-century Old Hall nor the fourteenth-century New Hall has survived intact, although the south wall of the New Hall with its distinctive and impressive hexagonal turrets is still standing. The surviving ground floor plan of the Priory as a whole consists of a medley of salvaged rooms and rooms open to the sky as garden courtyards. The restoration is well-designed, attractive and gives an idea of the size of the medieval Priory, if not of its life style. It was more like a comfortable manor house than a monastery: that much at least is apparent. There is one part of the building which is complete and has an authentic medieval atmosphere — the crypt, a dank, low-vaulted, brick-floored structure dating from 1300.

The crypt extends underneath the North-East Wing and part of the Well Court. Originally, there was probably a short under-ground passage leading north into the parish church. At the southern end of the crypt is a curious recess, which appears to be the beginning of an underground passage leading south but which has been sealed off. Immediately behind the stone casing of the passage on the west side, but not accessible from the passage, is the well shaft. The well is a fine one, lined with ancient bricks, sprouting ferns and covered with an iron grille. It descends a full 120 feet down into the chalk and there is even now fresh water at the bottom.

The parish church stands immediately to the north; the ten-foot gap between the buildings was originally bridged by a connecting passage, which may have continued as a pentise walk along the east front of the Priory. The monks were thus able to pass easily from the Priory into the church, whose relatively large chancel was specifically built as the monks' choir with stone benches along both sides; the nave was intended for the parishioners. It should perhaps be added that the Priory is the earlier building of the two, that the church was built principally to meet the needs of the Priory and that, in the early Middle Ages, the Prior was also the Rector.

This comfortable grange, which dominated the medieval parish, had its origins overseas. The mother foundation was the Norman Abbey of Grestain, near Honfleur on the left bank of the Seine estuary. Grestain was founded in 1050 by Herluin de Contaville. His wife Arlette had given birth to William the Conqueror while she was the mistress of Robert le Diable, Duke of Normandy. Robert le Diable, along with his descendents, the Plantagenet kings, claimed the Devil as his ancestor. The early years of Herluin's Abbey were troubled: it was on separate occasions both burned and sacked. Nevertheless, it became wealthy and powerful, largely as a result of produce garnered by its many satellite foundations, of which Wilmington was one.

The manor of Wilmington had belonged to Earl Godwin, but after the Conquest it passed, along with the entire Rape of Pevensey, into the hands of Herluin's dim-witted son, Robert de Mortain, who had fought with William at Hastings. Robert in turn gave Wilmington to Grestain Abbey. The Abbot of Grestain was no doubt grateful to have a base in Sussex so close to the sea; certainly his representatives in England were to find it a convenient headquarters. The first Priory at Wilmington was built in the twelfth century, although its early days are undocumented. In 1180, the extraordinary William Huband became fifth Abbot of Grestain and promptly left his Abbey to come over to England for a holiday of indefinite length. His indulgence in 'worldly occupations' led to admonitions and threats of excommunication from the Bishop of Lisieux. Whether the leisure-loving Abbot was staying at Wilmington Priory throughout this lapse is not known, but it is likely that he spent part of his sabbatical there.

During the thirteenth century, about thirty monks lived at Grestain and, somewhat surprisingly, only two at Wilmington. The first named Priors of Wilmington appear in documents at this time: Master Samson (1200), Prior John (1243), Prior Robert Pykard (1261), Prior William de Gymèges (1268) and Prior Reynold (1270).

In spite of the small size of the Priory, it exerted considerable influence over the surrounding area, controlling the agricultural output and pocketing a substantial proportion of the harvest. By the late Middle Ages, the inflow of wealth was such that the Prior built one of the largest tithe barns in the country. Its ground plan, 207 feet by 40 feet, can still be seen in the Priory car park. This magnificent barn was allowed to fall down in the 1940s, while in the possession of the Sussex Archaeological Trust.

The Priory exerted a different kind of power in 1315, when the resident at Milton Manor House was compelled by the Prior to build a chapel. Why Prior William insisted on this devotional act is not recorded, though perhaps there is a hint in the man's name, Paganus; he later became known as Paganus de Capella. His chapel is believed to have stood on the strange wooded mound called The Rookery, just south of the equally strange and empty site of Burlough Castle.

England's ambiguous relationship with France in the Middle Ages meant that at times of international tension the Alien Houses, as the foundations run from overseas were known, were subject to tight secular control. Clearly, it would not do for large quantities of produce or money to leave the country and pass directly into enemy hands. The first instance of confiscation occurred in 1295, when Edward I took possession of all the Alien Houses. It seems that the Prior of Wilmington may not have been ejected, though, since a document confirming his position dates from the following year. The Alien Houses were restored in 1297. In 1337, they were distrained again, this time by Edward III, and they remained crown property for twenty-three years. During that time, the estates belonging to the Alien Houses were used by the king at his own pleasure; the lands, cottages and the priories themselves were let out in order to generate revenue for the English Exchequer. Something strange happened at Wilmington. It remained untouched and, indeed, in 1343 Prior William de Bauville was officially exempted from exactions, charges and impositions for the remainder of the distraint.

The confiscation, which was only nominal in the case of Wilmington Priory, came to an end in 1360. The irregular war with France was going so well that the Alien Houses could be restored. Ironically, at the same time, English troops were sacking Grestain Abbey. Further seizures of Alien Houses followed in 1370, 1403 and finally in 1414, which marks the end of Grestain's control. Wilmington Priory was held for a century and a half by the Dean and Chapter of Chichester and run as a farm and vicarage. After that, in 1565, it passed finally into secular hands; it was owned first by Sir Richard Sackville and later by Spencer Compton, Earl of Wilmington.

How are we to interpret the Priory's ability to avoid distraint? For all the Alien Houses, inventories and valuations appear in the documents, so that both confiscation and restoration are recorded — and this applies even to those foundations that were able to buy themselves out of trouble by offering high tenders. But Wilmington Priory does not appear in the inventories at all. Did Wilmington hold some special status?

HERESY AND SORCERY
Medieval Christianity was a very wide Church. At the fringes it incorporated, sometimes resentfully, sometimes secretly, all manner of strange doctrines. Some of these heretical teachings were pagan in origin, such as the Cathar heresy; others were based on arcane teachings of the early Christians, the Gnostics, or on the secret writings of Judaism, the Kabbalah. All these heterogeneous beliefs were being disseminated in religious houses the length and breadth of Europe.

We have to acknowledge that in the medieval Church there was a broad and very blurred boundary between the corpus of accepted Christian thought on the one hand and the occult on the other. St Albertus Magnus (1193-1280) strongly supported alchemy and astrology, arguing that the stars and planets are the intermediaries of angels. St Thomas Aquinas (1225-1274) was taught by Albertus Magnus and shared his views; St Thomas was also reputed to have used occult powers to build a homunculus, which he employed as a servant. The automaton proved to be so talkative that St Thomas dismantled it. No doubt the story is untrue; the point is that it could be told by Aquinas' contemporaries without damaging his reputation as a saint and scholar. A later example of serious and profound involvement in the occult is seen in the career of Trithemius of Trittenheim (1462-1516). Trithemius wrote works on alchemy, magic talismans and the Kabbalah, and was a practising sorcerer. He was at the same time Abbot of a Benedictine monastery. The Abbey of Grestain and Wilmington Priory were also Benedictine foundations.

In 1500, then, a Benedictine Abbot could be a magician and write books about it. To judge from documented incidents, the atmosphere both at Grestain and at Wilmington was liberal enough for free thought to develop in the direction of heresy. The Benedictine 'discipline' at Wilmington Priory was virtually non-existent by comparison with the very severe discipline at Lewes Priory, which was a Cluniac foundation. A Cluniac monk always held up his habit so that his feet could be seen, always bowed his head in humility, never called anything his own except his parents, and kept perpetual silence in church, dormitory and kitchen. Breaking these or any of the other rules would mean public denunciation and flogging for the first offence; for subsequent offences, this treatment would be followed by incarceration for fifteen days in the Lantern, a tiny subterranean dungeon.

The mysterious south passage in the crypt at Wilmington Priory might, of course, have led to some dreadful oubliette: but I doubt it. The very small complement of Prior, two monks and five servants (in 1320) must have created an informal atmosphere, as would the continual ebb and flow of guests. Who were the guests who were so shunned and distrusted by the villagers? Some of them were certainly emissaries from the mother foundation in Normandy who were either resting after a channel crossing before setting off to inspect the other Grestain properties in England or relaxing before returning home. Were the others casual visitors or invited guests or a mixture of both? Given the worldly example set by some of his superiors, the Prior would have cultivated the society of neighbouring landowners, men with whom he had interests in common. Pevensey Castle was the nearest stronghold and it is curious that in 1254 Peter of Savoy, the Lord of Pevensey, should have shared the obligation to repair the ramparts of the castle with just twelve other men. Perhaps the total of thirteen men is not significant, but it is the number required for a coven and the number of lunar cycles in the calendar year. The Prior of Wilmington was among the thirteen, and he was the only ecclesiastical member of the group.

If, as now seems just possible, Wilmington Priory was a centre for some heretical cult, how would the Giant be involved in it, if at all? In order to know this, we need to discover what was in the minds of the celebrants. It is impossible at this distance of time to know what books found their way to Wilmington, and to know what books found favour there, but perhaps the most infamous and also the most feared and reviled kabbalistic work to be in circulation in the Middle Ages was the *Key of Solomon*. Witch-hunters, who greatly detested the book, referred to it as the 'Book of the Devil'; needless to say, it was widely and avidly read. It is thought that some of the ideas in the *Key* go back beyond Solomon to ancient Babylon, but like most occult traditions it grew by accretion and no part of it can be attributed to any one author — Solomon least of all. Yet it is possible that, to a superstitious and sensation-seeking community, the shadowy phantasm of Solomon himself seemed to be materializing from the side of Windover Hill. In this vision, the staves become the Pillars of the Temple;

[Solomon] made before the house two pillars of thirty and five cubits high, and the chapiter that was on the top of each of them was five cubits. And he made chains, as in the oracle, and put them on the heads of the pillars; and made an hundred pomegranates, and put them on the chains. And he reared up the pillars before the temple, one on the right hand, and the other on the left; and called the name of that on the right hand Jachin, and the name of that on the left Boaz.

(II Chronicles 3:15-17)

According to the measurements given in the Book of Chronicles, the height of the pillars with their capitals was between 60 and 73 feet: the length of the cubit varied slightly. Even so, it is clear that the Long Man's staves were not drawn to biblical specifications.

SOLOMON THE WISE, SAMSON THE STRONG
An alternative to this whole line of thought is the view that the Benedictine Prior, his monks, his servants and his visitors were quite conventional Christians. In that case, the Long Man might still have been seen as Solomon, but not the arcane and sinister magus lurking behind the eponymous handbook. Instead, he would

be transformed into the other Solomon, the great king to whom God said, 'Wisdom and knowledge is granted unto thee; and I will give thee riches, and wealth, and honour, such as none of the kings have had that have been before thee, neither shall any after thee have the like' (II Chronicles 1:12). Certainly the figure on the hillside appears triumphant, regal, supremely powerful and he is clasping what could easily be the Pillars of the Temple.

There is another biblical figure to whom this image would be equally applicable — Samson. Interpreted as the lion-slaying, Philistine-slaying hero, the Long Man takes on a new resonance. To a conventional, crucified Christ-oriented medieval community, the image of Samson would be seen as foreshadowing the humiliation, disfigurement, bondage and final self-immolation of Christ himself.

Call for Samson, that he may make us sport. And they called for Samson out of the prison house; and he made them sport: and they set him between the pillars . . . And Samson called unto the Lord, and said, O Lord God, remember me, I pray thee, and strengthen me, I pray thee, only this once, O God . . . And Samson took hold of the two middle pillars upon which the house stood, and on which it was borne up, of the one with his right hand, and of the other with his left. And Samson said, Let me die with the Philistines. And he bowed himself with all his might; and the house fell upon the lords, and upon all the people that were therein.

(Judges 16:25-30)

Heresy in medieval Wilmington remains a possibility that cannot be altogether eliminated, however bizarre it may sound, if only because it was a relatively common phenomenon. There is, for example, documentary evidence that the monks of an abbey in Lothian were indulging in unashamedly heathen practices in the twelfth and thirteenth centuries. The Lanercost Chronicle of 1268 records that a whole generation of monks was prepared to encourage the building of blatantly pagan idols and so corrupt the faith of the country folk of the area: 'Certain beastly men, monks in garb but not in mind, taught the country bumpkins in the neighbourhood to make fire by rubbing wood and to set up an image of Priapus; in this way they sought to succour the animals, there being an epidemic among the cattle at that time.' There is also the circumstantial evidence of Cerne Abbas in Dorset. The Abbey there was a Benedictine foundation, a sister institution of Wilmington Priory. Like the Priory, the Abbey at Cerne stands very close to a giant and it has been argued that both figures were carved by heretical monks.

Yet the documentary and circumstantial evidence for heretical beliefs and activities at Wilmington in the Middle Ages is too tenuous to put much reliance on it. Provisionally, at least, it would be wiser to see the Priory as an orthodox religious community. As such, the Prior and his monks would have tended to see the Long Man in terms of biblical references, whether to Solomon or to Samson is open to discussion. It may be significant in this context to remember that the name of the first known Prior was Samson.

That the monks themselves cut the figure in the hill side can really be discounted out of hand. The figure holds no obvious references to medieval stereotypes, and it is unlikely that such a public art work would depict a naked man. The idea of the Long Man as a pilgrim striding to Canterbury to pray at the shrine of St Thomas Becket can be discounted on the same score. This attractive notion came about because the Priory is close by, because pilgrims usually carried a staff for support and self-defence, and because the feet are turned to the east. As we have seen, the monks at the Priory might have used the Long Man as a subject for contemplation, but that is no reason to suppose that the monks made him. Pilgrims were usually drawn with *one* staff, which is a significant difference. The feet have been altered, so that the Giant appears to be walking to Eastbourne or Canterbury, but it was shown in Chapter 2 that the original outline had the Giant coming down the hill towards us.

The evidence for a medieval hand carving the Wilmington Giant is very slight. But is it possible that the Giant, who was on the side of Windover Hill during the Middle Ages, had any influence on medieval lore? In spite of the almost complete absence of any surviving local lore concerning the Giant, it is possible that resonances of the Giant and his setting may have found their way into medieval romances.

THE OGRE IN THE WOODS

S. F. Annett has suggested that the area centering on Windover Hill is the setting for an episode in the *Petit Saint Graal*, a story about Peredur, the son of Evrawc. In the paraphrase which follows, the features which refer to the setting of the Wilmington Giant are in italics.

Peredur, the hero, is on a quest when he comes upon a *castle with no inhabitants*. In the hall he finds a *chessboard on which the pieces are playing by themselves*. Peredur takes sides and inevitably loses; in anger he throws the chessboard out of the window into *the river*. An ill-favoured maiden enters and rebukes him but tells him that he can make good the injury he has done his host by repairing to *the nearby wood* and beheading the white hart that frequents it. Peredur rides into the wood, *hunts*, kills and beheads the hart. A mysterious knight seizes the head and carries it off. As a punishment for his failure, Peredur is sent to *a mound beneath which is carved the figure of a man*. There, he recites a spell and *a huge black man* springs out of the mound prepared to do battle. Peredur defeats him, and the black man disappears into the mound.

Some of the references are obvious. The mound is Windover Long Mound, the neolithic long barrow on the summit of Windover Hill. The carved figure beneath it is the Long Man. Less than a mile to the north-west of the Long Man, and flanked on one side by an old stream bed of the River Cuckmere, is a low mound called Burlough Castle. In spite of its name, there is not a trace of masonry anywhere on the site; nor is there any mention of Burlough Castle in any medieval documents. It is, in truth, a castle without inhabitants.

The Chessboard Castle of this story reappears in many guises in the romances as the mysterious castle where all kinds of strange and wonderful things happen, mystifying the hero. It is also known as the Bespelled Castle and the Castle of Wonders. Burlough Castle fits this aspect of the story as well, for it was long considered to be the home of the Sussex fairies.

The nearest wood to the carved figure and the deserted castle is the grove surrounding Lullington Church, three-quarters of a mile south of Burlough Castle. It is unusual to find a church in a wood, and Annett thinks this is a rare survival of a Celtic sacred grove. Such groves were provided with clearings where religious cere-monies took place and it is possible that the church — which is, incidentally, the smallest in England — was quite deliberately built on a pagan sacred site. The hunting of the hart may be commem-orated in 'Hunter's Burgh', the otherwise inexplicable name of a second long barrow half a mile from Windover Long Mound.

The idea that one or more of the great medieval poetic romances was set on and round Windover Hill is an attractive one. The furthest we could go would be to say that it is plausible and possible: no more. But who on earth is the wild man who springs out of the long barrow? The queens and princes, knights and squires of the romances are easy to understand as idealizations of virtues such as honour, duty, loyalty, chastity, tenacity and valour. The darker figures are sometimes difficult to understand. The treacherous Modred is easy enough, but there is something raw and uncontrolled in characters such as the ogre.

Atavism is the key. Let us look at a possible ancestry for the ogre who assails Peredur on Windover Hill. The Long Man was referred to as recently as the nineteenth century as the *Green* Man of Wilmington. The Green Man was one of the titles accorded to Merlin in his role as Man of the Woods or Giant Herdsman. Merlin's other aspect, that of the quaint and eccentric court magician at Camelot, is missing; here we have a figure who is nearer to Pan. He appears in some stories as an oracular and static figure, sitting on a mound in a clearing and surrounded by a variety of forest animals. When he appears to give guidance to the young knight Calogrenant in *Yvain*, Chrétien de Troyes' description of him, written about 1170, is grotesque rather than awe-inspiring:

I saw sitting on a stump, with a great club in his hand, a rustic lout, as black as a mulberry, indescribably big and hideous; indeed, so passing ugly was the creature that no word of mouth could do him justice. On drawing near to this fellow, I saw that his head was bigger than that of a horse or of any other beast; that his hair was in tufts, leaving his forehead bare for a width of more than two spans; that his ears were big and mossy, just like those of an elephant; his eyebrows were heavy and his face was flat; his eyes were those of an owl, and his nose was like a cat's; his jowls were split like a wolf, and his teeth were sharp and yellow like a wild boar's; his beard was black and his whiskers twisted; his chin merged into his chest and his backbone was long, but twisted and hunched. There he stood, leaning upon his club and accoutred in a strange garb, consisting not of cotton or of wool, but of the hides recently flayed from two bulls.

This seventeen-foot ogre, who is master of the wood and the animals in it, turns out to be knowledgeable, helpful and kind, in spite of his dreadful appearance. Although the grotesqueness of the ogre's appearance is characteristic of the medieval giant in general, his fundamentally Pan-like nature, carrying and protecting the wisdom of the forest, is a reference back to the Celtic god Cernunnos, who was also known as the Horned One or Herne the Hunter.

Is it, then, a dark and distant folk-memory of Herne the Hunter that keeps breaking the glittering surface of the medieval romance? It is very probable that the wild man who bursts out of the mound in the adventure of Peredur is a folk-memory of this kind — the involuntary resurgence of a powerful and irrepressible psychic archetype. It would be very appropriate if the all-but-forgotten prehistoric sanctity of the Windover Hill sites came to be connected with the Merlin-Herne ogre in the medieval imagination.

4. SAXON KINGS AND SAXON GODS

Faust: Where leads the way?
Mephistopheles: There's none! To the untrodden,
  Untreadable regions — the unforgotten
  And unforgettable — for which prepare!
  There are no bolts, no hatches to be lifted;
  Through endless solitudes you shall be drifted.

Goethe, *Faust.*

Apart from the supporters of the Benedictine monks, most of the people who have decided to go into print with their views have chosen a pre-Conquest origin for the Long Man. Some have suggested that he dates from immediately before the arrival of William the Conqueror, as the handiwork of King Harold.

HAROLD AND 'THE FIGHTING MAN'

Harold II, who reigned for only a few months in 1066, owned vast estates in England even before his accession to the throne. He has been described as the most powerful subject England has ever had. He was created Earl of East Anglia in 1045 and, although he was the younger son of Earl Godwin, his subsequent career was advanced incalculably by the irresponsible antics of his elder brother Sweyn. Sweyn it was who abducted and seduced a Mother Superior, the Abbess of Leominster. When it was apparent that the Abbess was with child, his offer of marriage was regarded as abhorrent by the Church and rejected out of hand. Disgraced and banished,

Sweyn no longer stood in Harold's way. The Earl Godwin himself choked to death on a crust of bread while banqueting with the king in 1053; Harold succeeded him as Earl of Wessex. In this way, he amassed vast estates.

Popular history depicts Harold as a forlorn and pathetic figure, a loser: but he was faced with the nearly impossible task of repelling simultaneous invasions on two widely separated shores, and recent European history has illustrated how over-taxing a war on two fronts can be. Harold was a great and courageous soldier; it was appropriate that his badge should be a warrior.

King Harold's personal standard, depicting the Fighting Man, ended up later that century among the treasures of the Vatican. Pope Gregory VII, as Hildebrand, had given William I support in his conquest of England and, in 1079, called on William to subordinate his temporal power to the spiritual control of Rome. William bluntly declared that he owed no fealty to Rome and as a brutal reminder that he relied on force to gain his ends he sent Harold's standard to Rome instead.

In his excellent outline of the principal Long Man theories, Sidgwick suggested that the hill figure might be a representation of King Harold's badge. He argued that, since the horse was the emblem chosen for the royal standards of Mercia and a line of white horses marks the approximate position of the Mercian frontier, the Long Man might be a similar boundary marker. The problem with this view is that neither Earl Godwin's lands nor Harold's stopped at Wilmington, so the choice of Windover Hill as a site for the badge has no apparent logic.

The Domesday Survey of 1086 does nevertheless reveal Wilmington as something of an oddity. The usual size of a Sussex hundred was between twelve and twenty square miles. Wilmington was surrounded by four hundreds, each of about twenty square miles; but Wilmington itself, together with the neighbouring village of Folkington, formed a separate unit of only five square miles, the Hundred of Avronelle. There was only one hundred in Sussex that was smaller than this in 1086, and that was Framfield, an island-hundred hemmed in on all sides by the Archbishop of Canterbury's Hundred of Malling; this vast strip-hundred stretched all the way from Firle Beacon to the Kent border. It is difficult to account for the special treatment accorded to Avronelle, except in terms of Robert de Mortain's gift of Wilmington to Grestain Abbey; because administered from Normandy, it would need to be distinguished from surrounding manors. It does not in any way point to Wilmington as a place held in special regard by King Harold.

THE WARRIOR AMULETS

The Saxons assimilated a good deal from Scandinavian culture and several writers have drawn attention to a picture on one of a group of bronze dies found at Torslunda in Sweden. These plaques were designed to fit into the front of a helmet, usually one above each temple, and they were invariably decorated with scenes of warfare.

The Torslunda plaque, which seems to relate to the Long Man, shows two figures. One is a warrior with partially extended arms, a horned helmet, a sword strapped to his back and two spears held more or less vertically. The legs are difficult to interpret: the figure could be kneeling or dancing. The fact that one spear is pointing up and the other down suggests a ritual dance. The second figure has been seen as a monster and certainly it has a monstrous, wolf-like head, but the rest of the figure is human. It carries a staff in its left hand and with its right it is drawing a sword.

It was customary for Scandinavian warriors to engage in ritual dances before going into battle. The modern parallels are obvious in, for example, the chants and songs of Rugby players and the highly ordered shouting, singing and clapping of football supporters. It is all part of the psychological preparation for contest, a device to make the adrenalin flow. The Norse warriors believed that during their war dances they turned into berserks, creatures who were half man and half savage beast. The two figures on the Torslunda plaque are really two aspects of the same man, the dancing warrior and the invincible berserk.

Although the Torslunda plaque has been mentioned repeatedly in the literature on the Long Man in support of a Norse-influenced Saxon origin, some other Scandinavian figures have so far been overlooked. One is a small silver amulet found at Birka in Sweden. In this amulet, the warrior stands symmetrically, with his hands outstretched and holding a sword in its scabbard in his left hand and what appears to be a staff in his right. The horns on the helmet curve inwards and meet at the top to enclose a hole for a thong; the amulet was worn as a pendant. A similar warrior amulet, in bronze, was found at Ekhammar, also in Sweden. The figure is again standing, not dancing, and holds a sword in his right hand and two short spears in his left. It is easy to see the Long Man as an enlarged version of these warrior amulets. The pose is right and the vertical weapons held in the outstretched arms are exactly right. Even the feet are turned in the same way as the amulets' feet; but we must remember that the altered feet of the Long Man are a false clue.

The form of the Swedish amulets is seen again in the Saxon buckle which was found in 1964 at Finglesham in Kent. This exceptionally well-preserved gilt-bronze buckle is closer to the Long Man in one important respect; apart from his helmet and buckled belt, the warrior is naked. The legs, curiously, are shown slightly bent at the knees, like those of a skier. The spears are shown converging towards the feet.

The links with the Long Man appear to be close, but where is the Long Man's horned helmet? The helmet is featured in exaggerated form on both of the amulets and on the buckle. Perhaps the horns were once there, but have been lost as the outline of the Giant became overgrown. A resistivity survey of a small area above the Giant's head was carried out by K. Gravett in 1969 (see Holden, 1971) to see whether the turf concealed any additional details. The

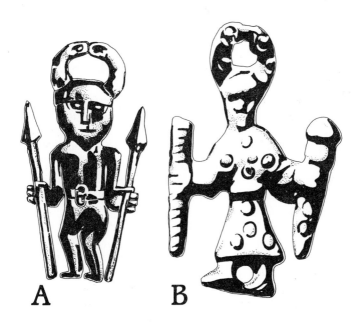

Figure 6. Saxon warrior amulets. A: detail of gilded bronze buckle found at Finglesham, Kent. B: silver pendant from Birka, Sweden.

only anomaly in soil depth to emerge was a single diagonal line leading upwards and to the left from the centre of the crown. In other words, possibly a single horn, but not two. The problem with this survey is that it covered too small an area to reveal anything coherent and convincing; the same limitation applies to the surveys carried out at the head of each stave. A background difficulty in interpreting resistivity surveys is that the anomalies are not diagnostic of buried outlines. Depressions may occur for geological rather than archaeological reasons. Conversely, some parts of the outline are not marked by any erosion of the bedrock surface.

So the matter of the horns must remain an open question. Nevertheless, in general terms, the concept of the Long Man as a large warrior amulet is an acceptable and reasonable one. As such, the Giant could presumably have been designed to give strength, courage and good fortune in battle to the South Saxon people. But why should it have been placed at Wilmington? Is there any reason why interest of this kind should focus on this block of East Sussex downland? I think there are two possible reasons, one relating to what might be called the middle period of Saxon history and the other to the earliest phase of Saxon colonization.

THE PALACE OF ALFRED THE GREAT

In the ninth century, when the power of the Saxons was at its height, the capital of Wessex was Winchester. But King Alfred, who reigned from AD 871 to 899, also possessed personal estates in Sussex and had some family connections with the county. Alfred's father, King Aethelwulf, was buried in the church at Steyning in 858. Burlough Castle has been ascribed, apocryphally, to King Alfred but there is a stronger association with nearby Alfriston and its unusually massive parish church, known by the nickname 'Cathedral of the Downs'. It is possible that the name of Alfriston is a corruption of 'Alfred's tun' or town.

One of Alfred's estates corresponded closely with the Hundred of Willendone of the Domesday Survey. This comprises the parishes of West Dean, Friston, East Dean, Jevington and Willingdon. On the estate, at West Dean, Alfred had one of his royal residences. There is nothing left of the palace, but it is thought to have been incorporated into West Dean Manor House, which is now completely ruined.

Alfred held court at West Dean and his first meeting with Bishop Asser, who later wrote the *Life of Alfred*, is known to have taken place there. Since the royal estate included all, or almost all, of the easternmost block of the Downs, it is possible that the Long Man was the northern boundary marker. At least that interpretation makes better sense than the alleged association with King Harold. But there is a third possibility: a third king with whom the hill could be connected.

AELLE, THE PIONEER KING

King Aelle was the first king of the South Saxons. We are told by the *Anglo-Saxon Chronicle*, written in the ninth century, that King Aelle invaded Sussex in AD 477. He landed at a place called Cymenesora, which is commonly identified as Keynor on Selsey Bill, with his three sons, Cymen, Wlencing and Cissa. In 491, the British fort of Andredesceaster (= Pevensey) was captured and all its defenders were killed. At an intermediate date, 485, Aelle fought the Battle of Mearcredesburna. Although this place has not been positively identified, the intermediate date is taken to indicate an intermediate position geographically, somewhere between Selsey and Pevensey. The meaning of the place-name is uncertain, but it appears to be composed of roots which mean 'sea-ford-river'. Given that the River Ouse is known to have had its mouth at Seaford until the sixteenth century, it looks as if the battle may have taken place between Newhaven and Seaford.

The scene that emerges from this interpretation of the *Anglo-Saxon Chronicle* is of a small-scale landing at Selsey — only three ships — followed by a slow and fiercely fought movement eastwards during which the Downs were cleared of Britons. The Long Man and the easternmost block of the Downs therefore did not come into the story until after the Battle of Mearcredesburna. Sidgwick suggests that, after the battle, Aelle continued north-eastwards, to clear the centre of the downland block behind Seaford, and then dropped down into the Cuckmere valley at Alfriston.

The undrained floodplain of the Cuckmere was marshy; naturally Aelle would select a crossing-place where the floodplain was at its narrowest. Alfriston was the obvious choice. The day of the crossing was also the best time for the local Britons to attack Aelle's forces, while the latter were preoccupied with the mire. So the likelihood is that there was a second battle as Aelle forced his way across the Cuckmere valley, even though it is not recorded in the *Chronicle*. This penultimate victory, for such it is assumed to have been by supporters of this theory, was commemorated by the carving of the Long Man. Thus the Giant, transformed yet again, becomes the triumphant chieftain Aelle, portrayed as the victor who is about to consolidate his position by sacking Pevensey and then declaring himself King of the South Saxons.

This narrative, climaxing as it does in the carving of the Long Man as a victory celebration, is a very appealing one, not least because it gives a firm date for the Long Man's creation. If the Battle of Mearcredesburna was fought in 485 and Pevensey was taken in 491, the scenario outlined above implies that the Long Man was made in perhaps 486, 487 or 488. It seems to solve the mystery so neatly. Unfortunately, there are problems with this traditional view of Aelle's invasion, and recent scholarship sees the episode in a different light altogether.

To begin with, the landing on Selsey and the identification of Cymenesora with Keynor are called into question (see Brandon, 1978). The 'seventh-century' document which mentions a 'Cumeneshora' is a later forgery made in support of a claim for territory. Since forged documents cannot be used as evidence for anything, we have to admit that the exact location of Aelle's landing is unknown. In addition, the reassuringly precise dates given in the *Chronicle* for early Saxon events are thought to be twenty years out. The landings probably occurred in about 445 and the assimilation of the Saxons was a more gradual process, without the genocide of the Celts pictured by earlier writers.

Still more important, the archaeological evidence shows that the earliest colonization of Sussex by the Saxons occurred in the downland block between the Ouse and the Cuckmere. Of the fifth-century Saxon cemeteries and settlement sites so far dated, five out of six are in the Ouse-Cuckmere block. Martin Welch has suggested that the reasons for this may be traced back to the Roman settlement of Sussex. In the Roman period, the villas and their estates were concentrated round the regional capital, Chichester, with a possible outlier at Newhaven. Thus, in the post-Roman period, there was a void in the eastern Downs. That the earliest Saxon sites occupy previously empty land and fit neatly into one downland block indicates a measure of sensitivity to the existing situation in Britain and probably immigration by licence.

The British were prepared to condone Saxon or Jutish colonization in return for military service. The earlier British King Vortigern made this mistake on an epic scale, by hiring an entire Jutish mercenary army under Hengest; in exchange for land, the

Jutes were to hold back the troublesome Scots. Vortigern was treacherously burnt to death in his castle on Hengest's orders. 'What hopeless stupidity! What dullness of intelligence!' railed Gildas, when he wrote his *History of Britain* in 550.

The same misguided trust allowed the South Saxons under Aelle to expand gradually outwards from their tiny power centre between the Ouse and the Cuckmere. The site of the Battle of Mearcredes-burna can still be taken as Seaford, though the battle may well have been fought against restless and resentful Britons from the west. The sacking of Pevensey was probably undertaken so that the eastern boundary of legal colonization, the River Cuckmere, might be crossed without any further hindrance. The second scenario, based as it is on dated sites, gives us a different perspective on the Long Man. The sacking of Pevensey opened up the entire downland block east of the Cuckmere and gave Aelle a solid, impregnable heartland from which his kingdom could expand to the west along the Downs and to the north, more slowly, into the Forest of Andredesleah.

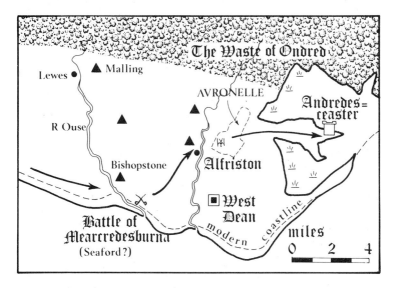

Figure 7. Map of Saxon East Sussex. The arrows show the traditional interpretation of Aelle's route to Pevensey, which was sacked in AD 470. The pyramids represent Saxon settlements firmly dated to the fifth century; these, the very earliest in Sussex, are clustered in the area between the Ouse and Cuckmere valleys.

If King Aelle was an astute tactician, and there can be little doubt that he was, he will have realized the significance of the fall of Pevensey. The Long Man might then have been cut in cognizance of the birth of his kingdom. The fall of Pevensey, dated 491 in the *Chronicle*, probably happened in 470; so, on this interpretation, the Long Man would date from AD 471 or 472. Whether the figure is Aelle himself or a stereotype of the South Saxon warrior, it can still be seen as a warrior amulet, the figure that recurs throughout the Saxon period.

BALDUR THE BEAUTIFUL

Although the Saxons later became Christian converts, the early generations of colonists were pagan, honouring several gods. If Aelle wished to express his victory enduringly, he might well have chosen to represent one of his gods. There is place-name evidence that several Teutonic gods were present in the Saxon consciousness:

Wootton, Wannock, Wadhurst	Woden/Odin	BATTLE
Thundersbarrow, Donnington	Thunor/Donar	THUNDER
Tye Oak, Tye Hill, Tyes	Tiw	DEATH?
Frieze Oak, Friezeland Wood	Frea/Freyr	FERTILITY
Loxwood, Loxfield	Loki	EVIL
Polhil	Baldur/Pol	SUN

Baldur, in his role as sun-god or summer-god, has been put forward as a possible identification for the Long Man. In order to understand fully the resonance of the Long Man, backwards and forwards through time, some understanding of the nature of Baldur is essential. In the Norse-Teutonic pantheon, Baldur was the best-loved of all the gods. He was the son of Odin, the chief god, and Frigga; his principal attributes were beauty, goodness and youth. Baldur dreamed that his life was in danger, so Frigga exacted an oath from birds, beasts, fire, water and a whole range of inanimate substances that none of them should harm him. The evil Loki discovered that the mistletoe had missed taking the oath, fashioned a dart out of mistletoe and persuaded the blind Hodur to throw it at Baldur. To the horror of all except Loki, Baldur fell dead.

Baldur's brother Hermod mounted Odin's eight-legged horse Sleipnir, which could outstrip the wind, and rode to the otherworld to plead that Baldur should be allowed to return to Asgard. He was told that this could only happen if everyone and everything should weep for Baldur. When Hermod returned to Asgard and reported all this, everyone and everything began to weep, except Loki, who was disguised as an old woman. So it was that Baldur was prevented from returning.

There are elements here, in the story of this short-lived, good-looking and good-natured youth, of a much earlier god of the sun or summer, whose brief period of power is inevitably brought to a close amid weeping. It is the same story as that of Ishtar's search for Tammuz in ancient Sumer, or the struggle between Aphrodite and Persephone to retrieve Adonis in ancient Greece. Baldur and Adonis were originally the same; Baldur, too, was won back again, to be lost again, only to be won back again, like the endless cycle of the seasons. The difference with the Baldur myth is that by AD 1200, when Snorri Sturluson came to write down the Edda, it had become a myth for adventuring Vikings who had lost touch with the cyclic ebb and flow of agricultural life. So the darkness and tragedy of Baldur's permanent exile to the underworld is a reflection of the Viking taste for the violent, morbid and tragic ending. Baldur seems also to look forward, or across, to the story of Jesus, who is the only rather than the favourite son of God; who, like Baldur, is youthful, pure, good and ultimately betrayed and killed out of spite.

If the Long Man is Baldur, the staves can only represent the leading edges of two doors. He is thus opening the doors of night to let day begin, or passing through the doors of winter to let the summer start. Or, most plangent of all, he may be saying his farewells to the other gods and closing the great doors of Asgard as he departs for the underworld.

ST WILFRID AND THE WANDERER

Aelle may, on the other hand, have selected Odin to commemorate his victory. As All-father, Odin saw and knew all that happened in the world. He also rewarded the brave warrior killed in battle with a place in Valhalla, the feast-hall for the Chosen Slain over which he presided. Odin as the Wanderer roams between the worlds with his hat, cloak and spear. In this role, he was sometimes known by the name Grim. It is hard to see how the Long Man could represent Grim. He is invariably represented with his spear-sceptre, but never with two. The only other possibility is the door image again. In this instance, it could only be the huge doors of Valhalla which the god is throwing open, welcoming the dead heroes and inciting the living to fight ever more recklessly in battle.

Whether or not the Long Man was made by the early Saxons, he can only have been interpreted by them in terms such as these. Paganism came with them in 450 and stayed, in certain pockets which resisted change, for two hundred years. There is a vivid description of St Wilfrid encountering a pagan community in Sussex. Wilfrid eventually became Bishop of Selsey in the 680s. Before this, in 666, he narrowly avoided shipwreck on the Sussex coast while crossing the Channel from France. The *Life of Wilfrid* by Eddius Stephanus, Wilfrid's chaplain and choirmaster, described the incident:

As they were sailing from Gaul over the English sea with Wilfrith, the bishop of blessed memory, the monks singing and chanting God's praise in chorus, a fearful storm arose amid the sea and, as with the disciples of Jesus on the Sea of Galilee, the winds were contrary. For, a great gale blowing from the south-east, the swelling waves threw them on the unknown coast of the South Saxons; the sea left the ship and men, retreating from the land leaving the shore uncovered, retired into the depths of the abyss.

And the heathen coming with a great army intended to take the ship, to divide the spoil of money, to take captives and to put to the sword those who resisted. To them our great bishop spoke gently and peaceably, offering much money, wishing to redeem their souls. But they with stern and cruel hearts like Pharaoh would not let the people of the Lord go, saying proudly that all the sea threw on the land became as much theirs as their own property.

And the idolatrous chief priest of the heathen ['princeps sacerdotum idolatriae', afterwards called 'magus'], standing on a lofty mound, strove like Balaam to curse the people of God and to bind their hands by his magic arts. Then one of the bishop's companions hurled a stone blessed by all the people of God, which struck the cursing magician in the forehead and pierced his brain, whom an unexpected death surprised, as it did Goliath, falling back a corpse.

The incident developed into a battle, during which only five of Wilfrid's men were lost. The saint prayed for an early tide, the ship was quickly refloated and made its way along the coast to Sandwich.

Now, if Wilfrid set sail from the French coast in the neighbourhood of Dieppe or Boulogne, and he was driven by a south-east wind, his journey would very likely have ended in the great tidal bay which has now become Pevensey Levels. Because Pevensey Bay was shallow, a falling tide would quickly have left the saint and his singing monks stranded on mud flats, far from the open sea and cut off from escape. This significant change in the coastline explains the apparently exaggerated description of the sea retiring to 'the depths of the abyss'.

If the stranding of St Wilfrid did indeed happen in what is now Pevensey Levels, the confrontation with the stern and cruel Saxons may have occurred as close as three miles from Wilmington. It is tempting to see Windover Hill as the lofty mound from which the magician cursed with fatal effect. And where else was the object of his idolatry, but graven on the hillside below him? Well written though it is, there is really too little in the way of topographic detail in Stephanus' narrative for us to be able to pin the incident down that closely.

Even so, the evidence in favour of a Saxon origin for the Long Man appears strong, multi-faceted and full of internal alternatives. He may be King Harold's Fighting Man, dating from 1050-1060, or King Alfred's insignia, dating from 871-899, or King Aelle's triumphant declaration of intent, dating from about 470. Alternatively, he may have been cut as a warrior amulet, or as a representation of Baldur or Odin, or more simply as a charm against the shot of wood-elves — at any time between 460 and 700. Of all these possibilities, it is the image of Aelle, the master strategist, the lost king with his vision of empire, that is the most vividly appealing.

It is a rich crop of viable alternatives; and yet there is something not quite right. The digging of one small trench across the outline of the Giant has thrown all these images of the Long Man's origins back into a turbid mist of uncertainty. The original outline of the Giant, marked on the solid chalk, is covered by a layer of chalk rubble and soil. The trench revealed, about halfway through this layer, an horizon of Roman or Romano-British potsherds. Not many, it must be admitted, but enough to show that the Giant was already basking on the hillside well before the Saxons landed.

5. VENI, VIDI

I have been in many shapes
Before I attained this congenial form;
I have been a word in a book:
I have been a light in a lantern:
I have knowledge of stars
That existed before the earth was made.
I have slept in a hundred islands:
I have dwelt in a hundred cities.
Learned Druids, do you prophesy of Arthur?
Or is it of something older?
Is it of me you sing?

Taliesin in *The Red Book of Hergest*, c. 1400.

THREE ROMAN EMPERORS

It was in 1937 that A. D. Passmore first noticed that the form of the Long Man grasping two symmetrically placed and vertical rods found an echo in the design of certain Roman coins. A brass denarius of the emperor Vetranio has an image on its reverse that is similar to the Giant, except that the emperor is clothed and each of the vertical rods supports a rectangular device or standard.

Vetranio is omitted from many lists of the Roman emperors, because his reign was so brief — only nine months in AD 350 — and because his rule was never acknowledged by the whole empire. The brevity of his reign seems to preclude him as a possible subject for a special portrait in outlying Britain, but he was not alone in using this pose on his coins. His contemporary, the emperor Constantius, was represented in the same way and he was in power for longer. Constantius was the son of Constantine. As a child, he was sent off to Gaul as a rather nominal 'Caesar', but he later held the countries of the East. On Constantine's death in AD 337, Constantius for a time ruled jointly with his two brothers Constans and Constantine II. A power struggle followed, and both Constantine and Constans were removed by 350. In that year, Vetranio assumed the purple for a few months, after which Constantius resumed control as sole ruler of an undivided empire. He died in 361, on the eve of a civil war with Julian.

In terms of personality and achievement, Constantius looks rather colourless. He was weak and fearful of his own generals. He was a conventional polytheist, but was liberal enough to permit the growing Christian community to consolidate its position. Although it is possible, there seems to be no cogent reason for Roman Britain to commemorate his reign.

A third and earlier emperor who used the Long Man pose on his coins was Antoninus Pius, who reigned from AD 138 to 161. Here at least is a name that is associated with Britain, but only because the defensive rampart in the Scottish lowlands was erected during his reign. The emperor himself never came to Britain; indeed, he never stirred outside Italy. His was a reign of gentle repose, by Roman standards. If any Roman emperor deserves to be remembered, it is Antoninus Pius. He was a mild man, a lover of justice and peace and under his benign rule tranquillity and order stole unobtrusively across Europe. Perhaps the Long Man is the emperor Antonine, or even the personification of empire itself.

To test the Roman theories concerning the Long Man, we need to look at the human geography of the Roman occupation. The most significant Roman site in East Sussex is undoubtedly the fortress at Pevensey. Standing on what was then a narrow peninsula commanding a broad and spacious harbour, not unlike Valletta, the fort consists of massive walls enclosing eight acres. The walls are twelve feet thick, as much as twenty-eight feet high and punctuated by ten bastions. The East Gate leads to the harbour, which was the site of Julius Caesar's landing in 55 BC and later became a major Roman port.

The distribution of Roman settlements in south Sussex was distinctly uneven. Taking the known towns, minor settlements, villas and other substantial buildings of the Roman period, there are thirty-three settlement sites west of Brighton and only three to the east. The villas, or Romano-British farms, are naturally clustered round the regional capital, the walled city of Chichester. The sites in East Sussex are a putative villa at Newhaven, a more certain villa at Eastbourne and the major shore-fort at Pevensey.

From Pevensey, a road pressed westwards, crossing the Cuckmere at Chilver Bridge and then continuing to Lewes. Troops marching along the road might well have seen the figure of the Long Man, but only if he had been kept scoured, as they would always have been at least two miles away from him. If the Romans had wanted to create such a figure, with the intention of impressing the natives and reassuring their own men, they could have found a better site. For example, the Long Man would have been more conspicuous and effective if it had been cut on the escarpment of the West Sussex downs, where Stane Street, the main road from London to Chichester, slants obliquely up the steep chalk hillside. There, the soldiers would have seen the figure in front of them and increasing in size as they marched towards it.

A STANDARD OF MEASUREMENT

There is nevertheless some evidence of Roman activity only three miles to the north-west of the Long Man, which could throw some light on the original function of the Long Man. In the fields surrounding the villages of Ripe and Chalvington, Ivan Margary (1965) has detected a rectangular, grid-like arrangement reminiscent of the centuriation that survives in southern European field patterns. Margary's long experience in recognizing Roman remains in Kent and Sussex enabled him to identify these fields and their hedgerows as a survival from Roman times.

The standard Roman unit of length was the *pes* (11.61 inches); 10 *pedes* made one *pertica* (9.67 feet); 12 *perticae* made one *actus* (116.1 feet), the major unit of land measurement. The standard unit of land area was the *jugerum*, which was two square *acti* or a rectangular plot measuring 240 Roman feet by 120. Fields laid out under a Roman agricultural scheme will thus have boundaries that are multiples of 120 Roman feet. Margary found that, even allowing for a certain amount of displacement after fifteen hundred years of continuous farming, the boundaries at Ripe and Chalvington still correspond closely with the Roman units.

The 'double square' of the Roman *jugerum* has similar proportions to the Long Man, if the extremities of the staves are taken as the four corners of a rectangle. The distance between the staves at the top of the figure is 116 feet 9 inches, which is very close to one *actus* (120 Roman feet = 116.1 English feet). The length of the staves is more difficult to measure; one is 232 feet, the other 235 feet, and neither may be its exact original length. Even so, 232 feet is remarkably close to the long side of a *jugerum* (240 Roman feet = 232.2 English feet).

This seems to show that the staves of the Long Man were used as a standard of land measurement, possibly referred to during the establishment of a colonization scheme or during subsequent boundary disputes. In this new transformation, the Long Man becomes an arbiter in Roman litigation, but there are two serious practical difficulties. One is the location of the figure on a hillside well above the farmed lowland. A site along the Lewes-Pevensey road would have been more accessible, and all that was really needed was a pair of marked stones set exactly 116.1 feet apart. The second problem is the shape of the figure. Although the staves are almost exactly one *actus* apart at the top, they are only 0.988 of an *actus* apart at the bottom. An error of 1.5 *pedes* would surely not have been tolerated.

So the staves do not, unfortunately, supply us with a simple pragmatic solution of the Long Man mystery. We are thrown back on the human form between the staves. Could it, after all, be an emperor? The weakness of this idea is the lack of convincing detail on the figure. He is naked; the figures on the coins are carefully dressed in all the accoutrements of the emperor in military uniform. The Giant's staves are unadorned; the *labara* held by the armoured emperor are elaborately decorated with discs below the level of the hands and surmounted by rectangular standards topped off by pommels. The Long Man, having no regalia, cannot be an emperor.

HERCULES REBORN

There is, however, one very telling argument in favour of the imperial idea, although it is an argument directed at another hill figure altogether. The Cerne Giant was identified by William Stukeley as a portrait of the emperor Commodus as long ago as 1746. If Stukeley can be proved right, it would provide some corroboration for a Roman origin for the Long Man, though not proof.

Commodus was the son of the emperor Marcus Aurelius and, although the boy was obviously unsuitable, Marcus allowed him to participate in the administration of the empire from the age of fourteen. The emperor lived for only four years after this, but it was long enough for him to regret what he had done. The beginning of Commodus' reign coincided with a period of peace and he was popular for a time, but an assassination attempt and the inevitable executions that followed gave him a taste for violence which progressively corrupted him.

He was told by sycophants that he could equal the achievements of Hercules who, by overpowering a lion and a wild boar and performing other feats, gained a place among the gods. Might not Commodus also be raised up? Wild animals were captured, brought to Rome and killed in the palace. Afterwards, Commodus took to displaying a club and lion skin beside his throne as part of his regalia and styled himself 'the Roman Hercules' on his coins. Once again flattery seduced him into performing these absurd and sadistic acts in the public amphitheatre, where he was politely applauded by a baffled crowd. During this display, Commodus murdered an ostrich, a panther, an elephant, a rhinoceros, a giraffe and several lions.

Worse was to come. Rome was indignant and ashamed when the emperor entered the arena as a gladiator. He, of course, played the *Secutor*, the gladiator armed with helmet and sword. His adversary, the *Retiarius*, had to fight naked with only a trident and net. The outcome was always the same: victory for Commodus. Encouraged by success, the emperor went on to repeat the performance seven hundred times. In public, the *Retiarius* was spared, but in the privacy of the palace, where some bouts took place, no mercy was shown.

Commodus was so delighted with this new role that he gave up the title of Roman Hercules in favour of 'Paulus', who was a famous professional *Secutor*. Commodus was regarded with disgust and contempt through most of the empire. His executions became so capricious that even his servants, concubines and lovers became anxious for their safety. Eventually, in AD 192, his favourite girl, Marcia, gave him some drugged wine and, as he fell unconscious, brought in a hired wrestler to strangle him.

The lurid career of Commodus was celebrated dutifully by ambitious or fearful courtiers in Rome, but it is unlikely that there would have been any pressure to celebrate it in Dorset, still less that there would have been any desire to do so. Commodus was interested in the diversions that Rome offered and avoided the discomforts of travel whenever possible. He was insistent that the statues of Apollo in Rome should be altered so that they bore his own head, but he would not have ordered a portrait hill figure to be marked out at Cerne Abbas.

The principal objection is really that it was not the Roman way to honour emperors — or indeed gods — in this fashion. If it had been, we can be sure that hill figures portraying Trajan, Hadrian, Nero, Claudius and a dozen others would litter the hillsides of Europe, and they do not. The hill figure is clearly a manifestation of an indigenous southern English culture, not an implant.

But what of the sherds of Roman pottery? There at least is tangible evidence of Roman activity on the figure of the Long Man. E. W. Holden (1971) thinks that they are good evidence that the Long Man was first cut by the Romans. The stratigraphy of the sections from which the sherds came offers some additional and very significant evidence that should modify that view. One Roman sherd was found above the outline of the eastern stave. It was not resting directly on the solid chalk, which must represent the first cutting of the figure, but in the chalk rubble and soil overlying it. The two inches of accumulated debris between the solid rock and the pottery fragment indicate that time elapsed between the cutting of the figure and the deposition of the fragment. The figure must, logically, be pre-Roman.

At a second site, on the Giant's right shoulder, several Roman (or Romano-British) pottery fragments form a layer seven inches above the solid chalk and parallel to it. In other words, a 7-inch layer of yellow-brown chalk rubble had masked the image before the Romans, or Romano-Britons, discarded their broken pots.

That they threw or dropped their rubbish on a monument to the indigenous culture implies a certain disdain. Nevertheless, if Roman troops marching along the road from Lewes to Pevensey could see the figure of the Long Man, it is likely that they were impressed by its size, simplicity and hieratic power. Although chalk rubble was accumulating on the outline, it may not have been entirely overgrown. The image could have been described in Rome and adopted for the imperial coinage.

The argument that Christianity was the official religion and that a pagan idol would be anathema is unconvincing. The trend towards Christianity was very irregular. As late as AD 363, the emperor Julian was reviving and re-establishing polytheism. In that context, it would have been quite easy for the Long Man image

to be assimilated. Its position only six miles from the port of
Pevensey may be very significant. As soldiers, merchants and
administrators made their way along the road to Pevensey, towards
the ships that would shortly take them home, the great forest of
Anderida (the Andredesleah of the Saxons) stretched away to the
left and the green crest of the Downs soared up to the right. One of
the last sights these men had of Britain before they returned to
Rome was the Long Man of Wilmington.

6. THE FIRES OF SACRIFICE

Mephistopheles: Here, take this key . . .
    Then to the depths! I could as well say heights:
    It's all the same. From the existent fleeing,
    Take the free world of forms for your delight,
    Rejoice in things that long have ceased from being.
    The busy brood will weave like coiling cloud,
    But swing your key to keep away the crowd!

Goethe, *Faust.*

If the Saxon and Romano-British periods will not yield the identity of the Wilmington Giant, there is a danger that it will vanish into the dusk. Documentary evidence inevitably decreases rapidly, petering out altogether in prehistory; archaeological evidence also becomes rarer as older features are obliterated by younger or by natural landscape processes. So it would be most satisfactory if the Giant turned out to belong to the Roman or post-Roman periods, because they are familiar. Yet convenience and familiarity cannot be criteria in the search for the Giant. If, in reality, he was the god of an alien and violent race, demanding horrifying ritual and bloody sacrifice, then it must be faced. Revulsion must not preclude an objective examination of all the possibilities, however unpleasant some might be.

IRON AGE HILL-FORTS AND ARTEFACTS
The seven hundred years preceding the Claudian invasion of AD 43

are known as the Iron Age. It was a turbulent period, with three major waves of cultural innovation: the Halstatt culture (700-400 BC), the La Tène culture (400-100 BC) and the Belgic culture (beginning 100 BC). Each of these changes involved influxes of peaceful migrants or determined invaders. Between times, there were local feuds and skirmishes over territory as immigrants tried to consolidate their gains.

In East Sussex, the volatile and uncertain situation produced a series of defensive hill-forts. Enclosures of three to ten acres were surrounded by at least one chalk rampart up to 11 feet high and a parallel ditch up to eight feet deep and v-shaped in cross section. The rampart was usually contained by a double palisade of stout wooden posts and broken by only one or two entrance-gaps.

The nearest complete Iron Age hill-fort to Wilmington is the one on the 490-foot summit of Mount Caburn. Its history began in about 500 BC, when an undefended farm was established there. The first, univallate defences were thrown up in some haste about 150 BC. The rampart was made of loose chalk without the usual timber revetment. It appears that the fort was attacked as soon as it was built, presumably by invading Belgae. The Belgic tribe, which then occupied Caburn as a permanent residence, equipped it with over a hundred granary pits and what seems to have been a water storage tank. The abortive expeditions of Julius Caesar in 55 and 54 BC were a signal to Celtic tribes all over the country to strengthen their fortifications. At Caburn, where precipitous slopes defend the site to east, south and west, only the northern side was strengthened significantly, with an extra rampart and a more substantial gate. But it was no use; the fort was attacked and reduced to ashes, probably by Roman troops.

Caburn was one of five major fortified hills along the South Downs, the others being Hollingbury, Cissbury, the Trundle and Old Winchester Hill. Of these, Cissbury was easily the largest, with an outer rampart a mile long and an enclosure of sixty-five acres; it functioned as a tribal refuge for a large region. Ironically, it was not needed as a refuge from the Romans. Cissbury was in the kingdom of the Atrebates, which included Hampshire and West Sussex, and which connived at the Claudian invasion under its quisling leader Cogidubnus. Apart from assuring and consolidating Cogidubnus' personal power and fortune, this strategy spared his citizens the mayhem that resulted from resistance.

East Sussex formed part of the Belgic kingdom of the Cantiaci,

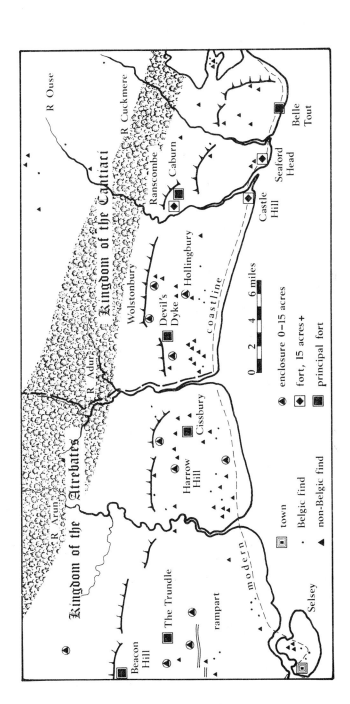

Figure 8. Map of Iron Age Sussex. The fortified enclosures were designed to give shelter to the people of the surrounding area in times of crisis. Farmers, their families and livestock could take refuge during tribal wars or foreign invasion.

which resisted the Roman invasion and suffered accordingly. Apart from Caburn, there were three other hill forts in the East Sussex downs, all of which were evidently sacked by the Romans, and which have been partly destroyed by subsequent marine erosion. The Castle Hill fort at Newhaven has been entirely destroyed by a combination of cliff retreat, artillery bombardment and the building of the nineteenth-century fort. Only half of the Seaford Head hill-fort is left perched on the cliffs between Newhaven and Cuckmere Haven. The same fate has befallen Belle Tout, on the cliffs south of the Long Man.

In the midst of all this political upheaval, the menace and the reality of invasion, the uncertainty and the massacres, it seems at first unlikely that people of the Iron Age had the time or the heart to produce works of art of any kind, still less on the scale of the Long Man. Yet, surprisingly, from all three phases of the Iron Age come art works of great beauty and refinement. The final, Belgic phase produced the bronze parade shield found at Battersea and the bronze helmet found at Waterloo Bridge. These were functional objects, but produced with such concern for decorative detail that they rank with the finest 'pure' art of subsequent periods.

The rough and unpredictable politics of the day had some effect on the Celts' general appearance, at least as seen by the over-fastidious and decadent eye of the Mediterranean historian. Diodorus of Sicily quotes a report by Posidonius, made in about 150 BC, that they were 'terrifying in appearance, with deep-sounding and very harsh voices . . . They wear a striking kind of clothing — tunics dyed and stained in various colours, and trousers, which they call *bracae*, and they wear striped cloaks . . . picked out with a variegated small check pattern. Their armour includes man-sized shields, decorated in individual fashion and on their heads they wear bronze helmets'. Now, although Diodorus is at first anxious to convey a conventional picture of the *macho* warrior, he gives more than a hint of a dandyish interest in clothes and accoutrements. Other contemporary reports and the archaeological remains themselves confirm this. They wore elaborately twisted and decorated torcs on their arms and wrists as well as round their necks. Tattooing was very popular. People of rank wore multi-coloured clothes bedizened with appliqué gold ornaments. Many different hair styles were to be seen and men's faces could be clean-shaven, moustached or bearded, according to individual taste. In a very real sense, the Iron Age in England is epitomized by

the elaborately decorated Desborough Mirror, dating from the time
of Christ.

Time was evidently available for the Iron Age Celts of East
Sussex to cut the figure of the Long Man, if they wished to do so,
and assuming for the moment that it had not already been created
for them. Whether such a figure would have fitted comfortably into
the Celtic pantheon is a more difficult question to answer.

THE DRUIDS AND THEIR SACRIFICES

References to the gods and ruling spirits of the Iron Age are
perilously few, and those few may well represent only a small local
cult or a short period of time, so that any generalizations about pre-
Roman Celtic religion are likely to be distortions of the truth. Even
so, it is clear that religion played a significant part in Iron Age life.
Caesar saw a threefold division in Belgic society: *plebes*, the
ordinary men who presumably got on with the farming and metal-
working, *equites*, the modish warriors and nobles, and *druides*, the
scholars and priests. It is now thought that Caesar's view of the
druids was a fanciful romanization; modern scholars feel it is
unlikely that druids taught reincarnation or held conferences on
the structure of the universe. Instead, it is thought, they performed
the role of witchdoctors, divining, prophesying and sacrificing to
their gods. Caesar was probably impressed by the large numbers of
young men crowding into the priestly caste, but the reason was
mundane: druids were exempt from tax and military service.

Caesar saw the druids as paler versions of Roman scholars, yet his
view seems not to square with other reports of Celtic druidical
activities. Both Tacitus and Cicero said that human sacrifices went
on and that the druids' altars ran with blood. Strabo wrote that
some sacrificial victims were stabbed in the back while the priests
made divinations from the details of their death-throes. Another
type of sacrifice was the votive sacrifice; an individual might be
decapitated and his head thrown down a well. Special cylindrical
shafts were dug for the purpose.

Undoubtedly the most horrific of the druids' rituals was the mass
sacrifice. It is mentioned by Strabo and Caesar himself describes it,
though without connecting the practice with the druids; 'The
Gauls [Britons] have figures of vast size, the limbs of which, formed
of osiers, they fill with living men; when this is set on fire the men
perish in the flames.' The description of a wickerwork giant, filled
with men and then set aflame has supplied the illustrator of

Britannia Antiqua Illustrata (Aylett Sammes, 1676) with a vivid image; his giant is some thirty-eight feet high with an unaccountably mild and ingratiating face. A later and more lurid version appeared in the *Saturday Magazine* of 1832, in which the Giant Druidical Idol was both drawn and described for popular sensation.

A link with the Wilmington Giant was first made by J. S. Phené, who was working on the problem of the Giant's origins in the 1860s and 1870s. The ideas from Phené's lectures were developed by St Croix, the man who made the first brick outline. St Croix, voicing Phené's views, pointed out that a large wickerwork giant would be a fundamentally weak structure, quite incapable of supporting the weight of dozens of men. As soon as the idol was lit, the wicker would have charred and disintegrated, allowing the sacrificial victims to escape.

Instead of a vertical image of a giant, Phené and St Croix suggested that a horizontal image was used. The outline of a giant was marked out on the ground by a wattle fence and the unfortunate victims were burned to death within the confines of the giant-shaped enclosure. The giant-shaped enclosure is, of course, the Wilmington Giant. Added force is given to this argument by the Giant's location, only six miles from Pevensey, Caesar's landing place. Caesar is certain to have seen this figure and may even have witnessed, first-hand, the rites connected with it. That, at least, is the substance of the Phené-St Croix argument.

One problem with this hypothesis is that, unless the victims in the enclosure were further confined in some way, for example by being manacled to iron stakes driven into the hillside, they might still escape when the wattle fence caught fire. Caesar does not mention any such refinement. Another problem is that the whole enterprise would be very difficult to manage on the north slope of Windover Hill. Its 28° gradient makes normal walking difficult. A complicated, repeatable rite involving the manhandling of prisoners, the building of a wooden palisade solid enough to thwart the victims' attempts to escape and the carrying of firewood to make bonfires inside the enclosure would be absurdly difficult on a slope of that steepness. There would, in addition, be every chance that both fences and bonfires would, once set on fire, collapse down the hillside, releasing the victims. The archaeological work on the site, slight though it has been, would have revealed signs of scorching and traces of charcoal over the outline. Needless to say, it has not.

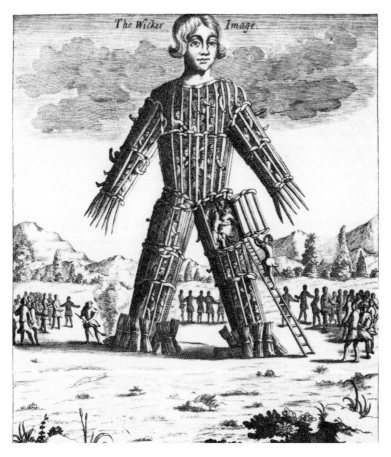

The Wicker Image.

Plate 2. The Wicker Giant. Iron Age Britons were said by Roman observers to have used gigantic wicker idols for mass sacrifice. Aylett Sammes suggested that the heathens did this 'to the Honour of their Gods and the mirth and jovialty of their Barbarous Spectators'.

It would be very satisfying if the origins of the Giant could be tied neatly in with classical documentation, but unfortunately the topography and archaeology of the hill figure make this explanation unlikely. So the vivid image of the flaming Giant, blazing away like a firework set-piece, seething with the victims' desperate struggle to free themselves and rending the acrid night air with their terrible screams, recedes, fades and quietens. We are left with the same Green Giant that mystified us at the beginning.

But this setback alone does not prevent the Long Man from being an Iron Age work. If the Giant is not the wicker giant of Strabo and Caesar, he may nevertheless be a representation of a Celtic hero or god. Since Celtic warriors in Homer's Greece commonly armed themselves with two spears, and the Irish Celts were armed in the same way as late as the seventh century AD, interpreting the Giant as a Celtic warrior-hero or war-god gives an automatic explanation for the staves.

GODS OF THE IRON AGE

The Celtic pantheon was very large, with gods or goddesses of fertility (Keridwen), springs (Grannos), war (Camulos), light (Lug), sky (Hu), sun (Beli), sea (Manannan), hot springs (Sul), fire and hearth (Brigit), strength (Ogmios), nature (Cernunnos), music (Mapona) and some three hundred more besides. In addition, there were limitless numbers of lesser, elemental spirits of earth, water, air, fire, plants and animals. Since the Wilmington Giant is raised up on a hillside and appears to be looking skywards, he may be Hu or Hesus, the sky-god. He carries spears and so may be Camulos, the god of war. He is seen to best advantage from the north and thus seems to indicate the sun's zenith; that would associate him with light, making him Lug, or with the sun, making him Beli.

There is some corroborative evidence connecting Lug with the Long Man, although the reasoning is admittedly tenuous. Associated with the far-journeying sun, Lug became linked in the Roman mind with Mercury, who was also a traveller. The Romans were eager to see equivalents to their own gods in alien cultures; so, through the Dark Ages, the ideas associated with Lug may have been assimilated by Mercury. The alchemical image of Mercury, which appears in the Renaissance, is symmetrical, with feet spread slightly and pointing downwards and with arms partially extended, just like the Giant. Unlike the Giant, Mercury has wings, hair and a crown, but he is holding a vertical rod in each hand. The staves are transformed yet again — this time into *caducei*. The *caduceus* is a wand with two snakes entwined round it, one spiralling clockwise, one anticlockwise. Normally the god is shown with a single wand: for alchemy he has two.

> He tooke *Caduceus* his snakie wand,
> With which the damned ghosts he governeth.

> (Spenser)

Even so, a more natural connection would be with the sun itself. If the Long Man was intended to point to the zenith of the sun's daily journey, then it is Beli who is marked on the hill side. The name was Latinized into Belenus and mentioned by Tertullian as being the principal deity of at least one Celtic state. It perhaps makes more sense in any case to connect a major image like the Long Man with what may have been the chief god of the region. But all this is very tenuous; the evidence connecting the Long Man with the Celtic gods is not at all strong.

There are nevertheless good reasons for believing the Uffington White Horse to be an Iron Age work. The Celts fought well on foot, but were fonder of fighting on horseback or from horse-drawn chariots. One of the most appealing aspects of their love of display was their gymnastic behaviour on the battlefield, where they performed carefully rehearsed 'feats' on chariots or horseback, to impress their adversaries. For hand-to-hand fighting, the best warriors practised alarming facial contortions. The horse, which was the focus of their martial arts, was accorded an honoured status and there is evidence of a horse-cult.

A bronze coin of the Belgic King Cunobelin, who became Shakespeare's Cymbeline, has a centaur on the obverse (British Museum); a gold stater, also of Cunobelin, has a galloping horse on the reverse (Ashmolean Museum). More telling still is a Belgic coin brought across the Channel by an immigrant entering Britain in about 57 BC. The reverse of this gold stater shows a stylized horse with a sweeping 's'-shaped body and legs which 'float' separately. The highly individual, exploded style of this numismatic horse is very reminiscent of the Uffington chalk horse, which seems to tell us that the White Horse was itself made in the late Iron Age.

The Cerne Giant might be Ogmios if he too belonged to the Celtic Pantheon. William Stukeley mentioned a Dorset tradition that he used to be called Helith, and it was noted earlier that the overgrown letters between his feet could be interpreted as 'ELID'. The alternative names do not preclude him from being Ogmios, the Celtic Hercules, since names and attributes varied somewhat with place and time.

The mythology of Iron Age Ireland reveals another Celtic deity who may be relevant to the problem. He is Daghda, a strange god with a whole string of attributes implying an ancient ancestry. Daghda was the Good God, the Great Father, the Mighty and Most

Learned One; yet in the narrative myths he comes across as grotesquely belligerent, grotesquely greedy and grotesquely virile. He clearly fits the image at Cerne Abbas, even to the club; Daghda included among his otherworldly equipment a magic cauldron, a magic harp and a great club. The 1979 resistivity survey of the Cerne Giant's left arm was generally interpreted as showing a lion-skin or cloak, but the disturbance on the chalk surface could equally be a shadowy relic of the magic harp of Daghda. Unfortunately, even if it could be proved conclusively that the Uffington and Cerne Abbas figures were both Iron Age in origin, it still would not prove an Iron Age date for the Wilmington Giant.

7. THE KINGDOM OF THE SUN

There is no other that knows you,
Save your son Ikhnaton.
You have made him wise
In your designs and in your might.

The Pharaoh Ikhnaton, 'Hymn to Aton', c. 1365 BC.

In rejecting the idea of a Roman origin for the Wilmington Giant and inquiring into pre-Roman possibilities, we did so knowing that there was a real risk of losing him altogether. Examining the Celtic possibilities revealed several likely roles for the hill figure, but the Iron Age offered no satisfying, substantial account of the Giant's origins. Even so, we might well be doubtful about pressing those origins back into the Bronze Age and neolithic eras, but for two very significant facts. First, one of archaeology's most distinguished figures, Sir William Flinders Petrie, has identified the Giant as probably Bronze Age in date. Second, there was a considerable degree of cultural continuity between the Bronze Age and the neolithic. Stonehenge, generally regarded as one of the two major monuments of English prehistory, was begun in the neolithic and completed, albeit in adapted form, in the Bronze Age. On these two counts, it is well worth making a careful examination of this remote era for signs of the Giant's beginnings.

BRONZE AGE BARROWS, BURIALS AND FARMS

Because there are so many threads of custom and practice connecting the two periods, it is difficult to put a date to the notional boundary separating the neolithic and the Bronze Age. The neolithic can be regarded as a native culture, and the Bronze Age traditionally begins with the immigration of the so-called 'Beaker' people, who came from the Rhine delta. They started settling eastern England in about 2300 BC; their culture is distinguished by the building of round barrows, in contrast to the neolithic long barrows, and the manufacture of flat-based pottery, as compared with the neolithic 'bag' or bowl pottery. There was a good deal of assimilation during this earliest phase, but the alien culture was more assertive after a second wave of immigration from the Rhine valley two hundred years later. A third wave, in 1700 BC, led to the establishment of an authentic Bronze Age aristocracy in the Wessex heartland: a league of chieftains powerful enough to control and exploit the native population.

It is probably most accurate to see the boundary in East Sussex as a four-hundred-year-long transition, stretching across the period 2100-1700 BC; but for convenience the millennium of 2000 BC can be used as the start of the Early Bronze Age.

Since we are leading towards the hypothesis that the Long Man is a Bronze Age cult figure, we need to look at Windover Hill in terms of the palaeo-geography of the Bronze Age. At first sight, the setting is promising. In his detailed study of Sussex in the Bronze Age, L. V. Grinsell (1931) observed that the county is very rich in finds of this period. Maps of findspots for both the Early and Middle Bronze Age, however, show a much higher density in the block of downland between the Arun and Adur than in the Ouse-Cuckmere or Cuckmere-Beachy Head blocks. If the Long Man was an Early or Middle Bronze Age cult figure, it was certainly not located at the centre of gravity of the Sussex culture. It need not have been, of course; it is quite possible that a sacred site was located on the periphery, where it might have been associated with the conjoint mysteries of sea, marsh and forest.

In the Late Bronze Age, the situation alters, in that there are now some seventeen findspots in the stretch of downs between the Ouse and Beachy Head, six of them in the same block as the Long Man. The main concentration of findspots remains the centre of the South Downs. But this line of argument is inconclusive. If the Long Man was clearly a central place in any part of the Bronze Age, we could argue that as proof that the Long Man was a cult-centre attracting or expressing high population density; if peripheral, we could argue that sanctity is often associated with the unfrequented lands marginal to the settled area. The dice are loaded in our favour, whatever we wish to prove. We can only make sense of the Long Man site in a Bronze Age context, if corroborative archaeological or ethnographic evidence emerges to show that the figure is consistent with other images or artefacts from the culture.

The amount of evidence for Bronze Age activity in the East Sussex downs is very great. The focus of Bronze Age culture in England as a whole was evidently the Stonehenge-Avebury area, and from here it spread into East Sussex along the chalk ridgeway surmounting the escarpment. On each side of this ancient track are enormous numbers of round barrows, most of which are Bronze Age; some 350 survive. It is thought that only important burials were honoured with barrows; it may be that the barrows were purposely built close to the track so that the spirits of the dead chieftains could go on guarding the traveller.

The barrows have yielded a wide range of artefacts: arrow-heads, knives, swords, spears, stone hammers, chisels, gouges, celts (axe-heads), beads, incense pots and cremation urns. Some of the more elaborate bronze celts, called palstaves, are both technically impressive and artistically satisfying, but the quality of the pottery is disappointing. By comparison with some of the earlier, native neolithic pottery from East Sussex, it is thick, crude and heavy with only rudimentary decoration. The most striking piece of pottery from the whole county is the great funerary urn found beside the trackway on Itford Hill and now in Lewes Museum; but this is impressive mainly because of its size, certainly not because of its finesse.

Close to the escarpment-top track with its chain of barrows are the remains of Bronze Age farmsteads. The closest excavated farm to the Long Man is the one on Itford Hill, six miles to the west. The great cremation urn was in a small cemetery on the crest of the escarpment. The farm, which is clearly associated with the cemetery, is about a hundred yards below on a warm, south-facing slope, and originally consisted of groups of circular wooden huts with clearly differentiated functions; some were living huts, others work huts, storage huts, stables and byres. The largest was twenty-five feet in diameter with a porch on the south-east. A curious feature, which we will come back to in a later chapter, is a chalk phallus which was buried beside the principal hut's door.

Leading away from the huts and their fenced paddocks, of which nothing now remains except a few post-holes, are the cultivation terraces or lynchets, which may represent the fields where the Bronze Age farmers grew their barley. The date of the lynchets is uncertain, as elsewhere on the Downs. Often they are casually referred to as Celtic; in fact it is very likely that some, perhaps many, were in use in the Bronze Age or even in the neolithic. On the south slope of Windover Hill, six hundred yards south of the Long Man, there are lynchets which Curwen (1928) refers to as being 'of Iron Age type': like so much else in these hills, they may well prove to be much older than has been thought hitherto. It is tempting, for example, to see the extensive system of small fields on the south slope of Combe Hill, two miles east of the Long Man, as contemporary with the neolithic camp or the Bronze Age barrows on the summit.

The general picture is one of widespread activity along the South Downs escarpment in the Bronze Age. Does Windover Hill mark any kind of focus to this activity? Certainly there are Bronze Age remains on and near the hill. The summit is capped by a fine ditched 'bowl' barrow that is 135 feet in diameter; unfortunately its shape is spoilt by a robber's pit dug into the centre. The robber in this case was Dr Gideon Mantell, who found a scraper, some broken urns and ashes: rather a disappointing haul. Some of the four remaining round barrows on Windover and its sister summit Wilmington Hill may also be Bronze Age. The lynchets to the south are uncertain evidence, but it does seem likely that a farming community was based on the area.

Below the escarpment at Wilmington there is clear evidence of industry. A hoard of bronze artefacts was deliberately buried for safe-keeping during an emergency and never retrieved, possibly because the bronze-founder was killed during a skirmish. It was re-discovered in 1877 and amounts to the richest hoard yet found in the area; it comprised one winged celt, twelve socketed celts and twenty-nine palstaves (all varieties of axe-head), secreted in an urn. Other hoards have been found at Brighton, Worthing, Newhaven, Lewes and Firle, so the Wilmington hoard is unique only in its size. It does nonetheless mark Wilmington out as a centre of Bronze Age culture. The orientation of many of the findspots along the scarp-crest as a great east-west axis of movement also tends to support the general idea of the Long Man as a piece of Bronze Age or neolithic artwork; the trackway passes along the skyline only forty yards above the Giant's head.

PHARAOHS AND PYRAMIDS

The style of drawing used to portray the Giant has a distinctly Egyptian resonance — a reminiscence, perhaps, of figures sculpted in bas-relief on the façade of an Egyptian temple. The Bronze Age and late neolithic in England were contemporary with the Egypt of the Pharaohs, so there is a possibility that the figure was cut by an Egyptian hand, or at least by an artist who had travelled to the Mediterranean and seen the hieratic temple art of the lower Nile valley. In his careful and otherwise quite comprehensive review of theories, Sidgwick (1939) did not consider the possibility that the Long Man might be Egyptian or Egyptian-influenced. As far as I know, the idea has not been put forward until now.

The Long Man has a simplicity and grace of outline suggesting ancient Egyptian representations of the human form. There is the hieratic posture, with the head and torso shown full-face and the legs in profile. The staves denote the office, rank or function of the figure and at the same time provide it with an implicit rectangular frame. The picture on the throne of Tutankhamun shows the young king kneeling sideways on a low stool, which makes the lower half of his body different from the Long Man, except that it is shown in profile; the arms and torso are similar, though, with hands grasping vertical parallel rods, which form a frame to the king's portrait. The throne-back is surmounted by a winged disc representing the moving sun. Tutankhamun's crown represents a sun-disc. The wands he holds in his hands are topped by smaller sun-discs. Is it possible that the Long Man's staves were once embellished in the same way?

Contact between Bronze Age southern England and the Mediterranean cultures of the period has been proved. At Stonehenge in 1953, Professor Atkinson discovered a carving on Stone 53; it appeared to be a representation of a dagger of the type which was in use in Mycenae in about 1600 BC (Balfour, 1979). In a bowl-barrow close to Stonehenge, a shale bead was found in the shape of a double-axe, a symbol often associated with Minoan Crete (Dyer, 1973). If there was communication, perhaps even trade, between Wessex and the eastern Mediterranean, ideas for the design of the Long Man could have penetrated from Egypt to East Sussex at the same time.

It is well-known that the Pharaohs had a taste for the gigantic. The great temples at Luxor, the Sphinx and pyramids at Gizeh and the temple at Abu Simbel all bear witness to an addiction to the colossal, presumably as an expression of naked power. The Giant, too, is a colossal figure and relates itself naturally to other figures of colossal conception. This is a strong argument in favour of a Bronze Age — or perhaps neolithic — origin. In Celtic, Romano-British and Saxon England, power was not expressed simply by largeness of scale.

Reinforcing this interpretation, there are one or two detailed features of the Giant that seem to relate it to ancient Egypt. The Great Pyramid of Cheops, which was built in about 2600 BC, has been surveyed more exactly than any other building in the world, largely because it has long been believed that the dimensions of its chambers and passages carry encoded histories and prophecies of great significance (Lemesurier, 1977). Its shape is known very precisely and, although its capstone is missing, it is possible to calculate the original height of the complete structure: 480½ feet.

My own calculation of the Long Man's original height, allowing for the 1874 alteration to the legs, was 240 feet, a figure arrived at independently of Horsfield's 240 feet quoted in his *History of Sussex* (1835). The original Long Man was thus exactly half the height of the complete Pyramid. This can, of course, be dismissed as mere coincidence and we must take care to avoid the absurdities that can result when the 'numbers game' is taken to extremes.

The ancient Egyptians did not use imperial feet and inches, but cubits and primitive inches. The primitive inch is agreed to be equivalent to 1.00106 imperial inches and is sometimes called the Pyramid Inch. The cubit is more problematical. The Royal Cubit (RC) is 20.63 imperial inches or 1.719 feet, while the Sacred Cubit (SC) is 25.0265 imperial inches or 2.0855 feet (Lemesurier, 1977). Assuming that the Pyramid design operates in round numbers, either Royal or Sacred Cubits could have been used to produce a pyramid of that height, since it is 280 RC and 230 SC.

To find out whether any of these units were used in laying out the Long Man, we can convert the length of the original figure and the distance between the staves.

	Height of Pyramid	Height of Long Man	Long Man Width: top	Long Man Width: bottom
Feet	480.5	240.0	116.75	114.67
RC	279.5	139.6	67.9	66.7
SC	230.4	115.1	56.0	55.0

The table shows clearly that the best-fit conversion is to Sacred Cubits. The Long Man is 115 SC high and the width of the figure tapers, by one Sacred Cubit, from 56 SC at the top to 55 SC at the bottom. The fact that these three dimensions — the main dimensions — of the Long Man are apparently in units used in ancient Egypt in 2600 BC is highly suggestive but certainly not conclusive.

Even if some common unit of measurement is proved, no other cultural link with Egypt can be positively proved from the figure. The twisting of the legs into profile is a late Victorian feature. As we saw in Chapter 2, the legs were originally shown frontally with the feet pointing downwards and outwards. This significantly alters the whole mien of the figure, making it far less 'Egyptian'.

Although it now seems unlikely that the Long Man is the work of an Egyptian hand, or even the conception of a Mediterranean mind, it is worth remembering that the figure is measurable in Sacred Cubits, which were in use in 2600 BC, and that the people who made the Long Man were impressed by the colossal. The idea of the sun-god or sun-king is another powerful idea to retain. The Giant's north-facing aspect intends the viewer to face due south, the direction from which the sun's full power comes. Though not an *Egyptian* sun-god, he is likely to be a sun-god nonetheless.

THE BOHUSLÄN GIANT

No one has pointed to the Mediterranean before in search of the Giant's origins, but Sidgwick and Petrie both indicated that northern Europe may have produced the image indigenously. Sidgwick mentions that there are, admittedly smaller, rock carvings similar to the Long Man on the shores of Lake Onega, close to the Finnish border in Russia. These are Bronze Age in date.

There are more carvings of the same type, also Bronze Age, in Scandinavia. On a flat rock surface at Bohuslän in Sweden is a figure bearing a striking resemblance, not to the Wilmington Giant, but to the Cerne Giant. The Bohuslän Giant is seen in profile, apart from his shoulder girdle which is shown frontally. Like the Cerne Giant he is shown with erect phallus; like the Cerne Giant he is brandishing a weapon, which he holds diagonally above his right shoulder — in this case, it is a spear with a huge diamond shaped tip. The right arm, holding the spear, is partially extended. The left arm is also partially extended, but seems to be holding nothing. So the position of the arms at least is reminiscent of the Wilmington Giant.

The Bohuslän Giant may be a representation of Tiwaz, who played a double role in the primitive Germanic pantheon, as both supreme sky-god and Ruler of the Battlefield. His association with the fructifying sun and rain may explain why he is shown as a fertility god; the menacing gestures he makes with his arms show his warlike aspect. Is this — at last — the identity of the Cerne Giant, that we have stumbled upon?

Brian Branston (1974) has tentatively identified the primitive deities of North-west Europe as Tiwaz the sky-god, Wodenaz the air-god and Nerthus the earth-god or -goddess. These identifications are still very uncertain; but if the Cerne Giant is Tiwaz, we may be close to discovering the identity of the Wilmington Giant.

VARUNA, AN INDO-EUROPEAN SKY-GOD

We come now to the work of Sir William Flinders Petrie, whose work on neolithic and Bronze Age sites in England and overseas is uniquely distinguished. In 1880, when he was thirty-three, Petrie published his *Stonehenge: Plans, Descriptions and Theories*; it contained the results of his survey of the great stone circle, which is still held to be the most accurate ever undertaken. In it, he gave the famous stones the scheme of numbers that archaeologists still use. On finishing this classic survey, Petrie went to Egypt to conduct another, of the Great Pyramid of Gizeh. The expedition was partly inspired by his father's obsession with the ideas of Charles Piazzi Smyth, the Astronomer Royal of Scotland, who attributed profound importance to the dimensions of the Pyramid. Petrie's survey, however, revealed the unsoundness of Smyth's theories; once again, Petrie completed a survey the accuracy of which has not been surpassed.

Later, in 1922, Petrie undertook an investigation of that English near-pyramid, Silbury Hill. This time he was less successful: he expected Silbury to contain a burial chamber but failed to find any kind of entrance passage. Nevertheless, the exceptionally careful approach which Petrie brought to bear on Stonehenge and the Great Pyramid obliges us to look very carefully at his work on the Long Man. In 1926, he published his paper on 'The Hill Figures of England', which included the first — I think the only — survey of the Long Man and a brief discussion of the figure's origin.

One peculiarity of the Long Man Petrie noticed, and which no-one else has ever mentioned, is the existence, in the turf, of facial features. The eyes are marked by hollows, the nose is a boss with recesses for nostrils and the lips are seen as a long boss of turf. How reliable Petrie's observations were can be judged by his brilliant and apparently impeccable record, but it must be said that there is absolutely no trace of any features in the turf now and it seems unlikely that there were in the mid-1920s.

Petrie's view of the Long Man's origins are much more significant, especially since he alone of the serious writers on the subject has put those origins so far back in time. Petrie felt that it was a Bronze Age figure and that it was a god, probably in the act of opening the Gates of Heaven or the Gates of the Underworld. As to the specific identity of the god, Petrie suggested Varuna, who was worshipped in Asia and European Russia in the Bronze Age and who was probably imported by immigrant Beaker people.

Three separate arguments were put forward in favour of this identification. First, Varuna is traditionally represented opening the Gates of Heaven, which agrees with the general design of the Long Man. Second, the Long Man is placed in a coombe so that it is in shadow at sunrise and sunset for ten months consecutively, and Varuna was a god of gestation. Third, the Long Man faces north, the region ruled by Varuna.

There are excellent reasons for supporting any interpretation made by Flinders Petrie; he was a man superbly fitted by his earlier work on Stonehenge, the Great Pyramid and Silbury Hill to unravel the knotty problem of the Long Man's identity. But we must not be overawed. Side by side with his excellent survey of Stonehenge came the commentary in which he observed that the monument was laid out in units of 11.645 inches, the Roman *pes*. As a result, he believed Stonehenge to be a post-Roman edifice. In addition, he made errors in calculating changes in the positions of past midsummer sunrises and accordingly gave Stonehenge a date of AD 730, plus or minus 200 years, which is the latest date ever proposed.

Petrie was fallible. It seems as if he may have been wrong in identifying the Long Man as Varuna. Varuna does indeed have a sky-god aspect, but rather a specialized one. *Varunas* is the Sanskrit word for night-sky and the root *var*, to cover, gave rise to the god's name. When Varuna was taken to Greece by the Achaeans in 1900 BC, the night association was dropped, and so was the god's separate identity. Instead a unified triple goddess, Ana, supervened. So Varuna ruled over night only. His other aspect, as a sea-god, appears to have been more important. He was known in Asia

Minor in 1400 BC as one of the male trinity of gods: Mitra
(= Zeus), Indra (= Hades) and Varuna (= Poseidon).

Far from usually being represented opening the Gates of Heaven,
he is normally shown *seated* on a sea monster known as Makara; as
such he is the god of the waters. The Vedic pantheon, to which
Varuna belongs, resides on Mount Meru, a mythical mountain at
the centre of the world, and Varuna is lord of the *western* quarter of
Mount Meru, not the northern.

Further, the human gestation period is nine months, not ten, so
the ten months of shadow at sunrise and sunset noted by Petrie at
the Long Man cannot be held to signify pregnancy. Even that link
with Varuna disintegrates under examination.

The whole idea of a distant Vedic origin for the Long Man is
unconvincing. There are too many geographical, historical and
mythological links missing. If a Vedic origin is accepted, along with
it we have to accept on trust too many unseen and unproven transformations in both the figure and the myth. For it is a myth we are
seeking. That much at least is clear from the journey we have made
so far. Not just a hero, not just a god lost in time and space — but an
entire myth. It is here that we take the final step back in time, across
the long transition into the neolithic.

8. DEATH RITES AND ETERNITY

When you set in the western horizon of the sky,
The earth is in darkness like death.
They sleep in their chambers,
Their heads wrapped,
Their nostrils stopped,
None seeing the other,
While all their things are stolen.
And they know it not.

The Pharaoh Ikhnaton, 'Hymn to Aton', c. 1365 BC.

MAGIC AND MAN'S DOMINION OVER NATURE

The neolithic age was an age of adventurous pioneering. The highly mobile hunting bands of the upper palaeolithic were well-organized and well-equipped; they had proved their fitness to survive through the many vicissitudes of the Ice Age. Yet they suffered from excessive dependence on the migrations of the creatures they hunted. Neolithic man solved the problem by capturing, penning and breeding the animals that met his needs. The domestication of livestock meant that he could be sure of meat and milk when he wanted them. His diet was improved by the domestication of plants; by sowing the seeds of edible vegetables, fruits and cereals, he could be sure that he never went hungry. An important side-effect of these activities was a settled life style. The farmer was no longer forced to go on endless journeys hunting and gathering, because he had arranged for all the essential foods to grow near his home. Conversely, the livestock had to be protected from predation by wild animals, fed and watered, while the arable fields needed ploughing, sowing, weeding and harvesting; so the farm effectively *kept* neolithic man in one place.

The neolithic farmers were attempting to create and control a microcosm of nature at large, selecting those elements that suited them, excluding those that did not. They were aware of the *hubris* implicit in their action and did their utmost to enlist the sympathy and support of their gods, the ruling spirits of the natural world. They were not the first to use magic to assist their economy. The old stone age hunters were apparently employing some kind of hunting magic when they decorated their cave-shelters with careful drawings of bison, horse, mammoth and stag. It may, as recent work suggests, have been more complicated than merely willing the animals portrayed to fall into the hunter's hands (Hadingham, 1979). Even so, some kind of sympathetic magic was clearly involved.

Figure 9. Neolithic farming. This rock engraving from the Val Camonica in Italy shows ploughing with an ard drawn by two oxen and harvesting with sickles, *c*.2000 BC.

The rituals and monuments of neolithic man were geared to essentially the same end: the winning over of those natural forces required to yield adequate supplies of food. One important change in the neolithic was that the farmers saw the need for a *gestalt* approach to nature. They realized it was not enough to will the appearance of grain, milk and meat. Instead the earth had to be watered by rains and warmed by the sun; the seasons had to follow one another in due sequence; man himself had his own part to play in ploughing, sowing and harvesting at precisely the right times. Nature was recognized as an intricate and complex mechanism, while food production was seen to be a precariously balanced partnership between man and the forces of nature. Add this *gestalt* view to the settled way of life adopted by the neolithic farmers and the path is clear towards the development of elaborate and complex rituals and the establishment of fixed cult centres, first of local, then of regional importance.

What neolithic man felt about his great and adventurous experiment with agriculture can only be guessed. To twentieth-century man, habituated to the idea of five millennia of continuous agriculture, it may seem a commonplace activity, an obvious and natural way of obtaining food. But to neolithic man it was a new and daring venture, full of uncertainty; every part of the process had to be worked or willed, including the passage of the seasons. Was he made nervous and fearful by his *hubris*, or was he intoxicated by it? We can interpret the large and potent monuments he made as evidence in either direction; certainly he was aware of the vast power he was harnessing.

THE CHAMBERED TOMBS

One powerful image with which neolithic man concerned himself was that of death followed by regeneration. Since there is a neolithic cenotaph overlooking and dominating the site of the Long Man, the neolithic idea of death needs to be explored in some detail. Although all the cenotaphs in Sussex are solid earth barrows, the concept behind them is most easily understood by approaching them through the literally more accessible chambered tombs of other parts of Britain.

In highland Britain, where hard rocks are plentiful, it was easy to build a simple chamber or room out of slabs of rock, a little house for the dead, before piling rubble and earth on top to make a mound. Using the same method, it was a relatively simple matter to build a passageway from the chamber to the exterior. Two flat slabs were planted vertically in the earth and a third, the roof-stone, was laid on top; the pattern could be repeated endlessly. In this way, the great passage-graves of the north were built.

The walls in the passage-grave of New Grange were carefully carved with spirals, representing the journey into the self. For the dead, the spiral represents the journey to or even through the underworld; for the living, who visited the dead by passing along the open passage, it represents the journey of self-discovery and self-realization. The New Grange passage penetrates only 65 feet into the great mound before it reaches the tiny square chamber with its three funerary niches. The scale of the little charnel house is dis-

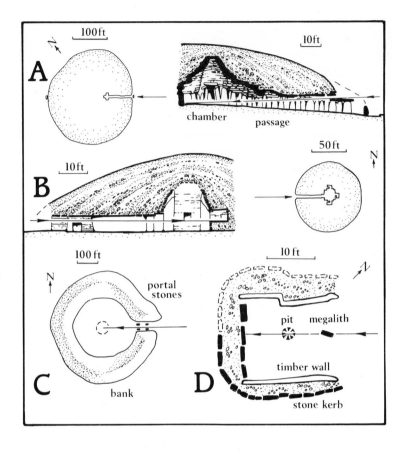

Figure 10. Solar orientations in neolithic tombs and temples. A: plan and section of New Grange. The passage was built such that the first rays of the midwinter sunrise lit up the central chamber. B: section and plan of Maes Howe, Orkney, oriented to the equinox sunset. C: plan of Mayburgh, Yorkshire. The entrance was arranged so that the equinox sunrise was seen through two pairs of portal stones. D: plan of the cult house at Tustrup, Denmark. Like Stonehenge I, this temple is oriented to the midsummer sunrise.

appointing by comparison with the grandeur of the great hemispherical mound that covers it, 260 feet in diameter. With its veneer of glistening quartz intact and shimmering in the summer sun when it was completed in 3300 BC, the exterior must have been a spectacular sight. Even now, after its recent partial restoration, it is a very impressive monument.

The disparity between external appearance and internal contents is easily understood. The great megalithic tombs are not tombs of chieftains or of any other individuals. They were clearing houses or waiting rooms through which people passed on their way from life to afterlife. The newly dead were either temporarily buried or exposed for a year or so, until the flesh had decayed, and then the bones were gathered up and stored in the tomb. After long periods had elapsed and the chambers filled to overflowing, they were cleared out, the older bones having lost their link with the spirits that once possessed them.

It is a different concept of the grave from the modern one. Today, the grave is a personal possession. Yet it is not so long ago that the great majority of people were buried in unmarked graves. My own great-grandparents have unmarked graves and so it was, I believe, with all their ancestors before them. The medieval churchyard was a large common grave with the coffins of strangers, often several generations apart, piled three deep in the ground. It is no accident that ancient churchyards appear in the landscape as raised platforms.

Figure 11.   The triple spiral, New Grange, County Meath. This rock engraving is in the central chamber of the passage grave. See also *Figures 10* and *23.*

The megalithic passage-grave has something of that commonalty. Unlike the Great Pyramid of Cheops, New Grange cannot be identified as the tomb of a mighty and powerful king. Instead it is a monument to Death itself, affirming the important truth that life and death are two continua, two modes of being that continually intertwine. In dying, man becomes earth. The earth shapes itself into new life. The cycle repeats endlessly.

It was inevitable that neolithic man should seize on this concept, since he was for the first time dependent on the fertility of the soil and its yield at harvest time. He could see his own death and the decay of his own body in relation to soil fertility. He could use the gesture of surrendering his body as an earnest that he was prepared to commit himself to the uttermost in the common project.

BIRTH, DEATH AND THE EARTH GODDESS
The relationship between man and earth is the beginning of the myth. Like a mother, the earth gives birth to us, feeds us, nurtures us and causes us to grow. At that point, the myth evolves beyond the metaphor; the Earth Mother needs to be repaid with offerings, whether in gratitude or propitiation, in order to ensure that the nurture continues. The final and most potent offering is the surrender of our own earthly bodies for reincorporation into the substance of the Earth Mother.

Burial in the chambered tomb or in the solid earth of the long barrow was thus the central symbolic act of neolithic faith. It implies confidence and trust that the cycle of life will begin again. The rounded, hemispherical mounds covering the passage-graves are reminiscent of the bellies of the figurines representing the pregnant fertility goddess. Some, like the bottle-shaped amulet of the goddess found at Sitagoi in Macedonia, have a spiral or inter-locked double-spiral maze marked on their bellies: these are variations on the same spiral maze that is marked on the stone at the centre of New Grange.

The double-spiral maze is a visual analogue of the physical and spiritual journey which was thought, on a local level, to attend the death rites and, on a wider level, to be ensured by the death-monuments for the landscape at large. Dying, we enter the maze; re-emerging, we are reborn. The siting of the tombs and barrows, dominating the rural scene, shows that their regenerative power was intended to permeate whole regions.

Portraits, or rather conceptual models, of the Earth Mother have been found at many sites both in Britain and on the mainland of Europe. Usually she is shown with grotesquely exaggerated hips and belly to emphasize her birth-giving function. Professor Gimbutas sees the Great Goddess as a supreme creator, giving birth from her own substance unaided by any other being (Gimbutas,1974). This 'virgin' aspect is thought to have been carried over into later goddesses such as Artemis, and presumably even reappears as late as the immaculate mother of Christ. Gimbutas feels that the goddess who conceives by interaction with a sky-god is a later, Indo-European version of the Great Goddess. Whether that is so or not, the figurines of the Earth Mother found in Britain are associated with phalli carved out of chalk or bone. This implies that, in Britain at any rate, she was not thought of as a virgin goddess.

In spite of Gimbutas' belief that there is no evidence that neolithic man understood the connection between sex and conception, the juxtaposition of pregnant female figurines and phalli at sites such as Grimes' Graves provides just that evidence. This in turn implies that neolithic religion was not strictly monotheistic.

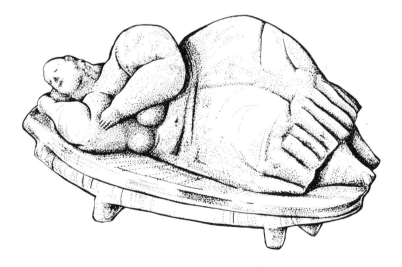

Figure 12. The neolithic earth-goddess, *c*.2500 BC. The 'Sleeping Lady' figurine was found in the Hypogeum, a subterranean temple cut out of the living rock at Paola near Valletta, Malta.

Worship of the Great Goddess, the Earth Mother, no doubt dominated; but there was certainly also recognition of a masculine principle at work in creation.

Indeed, the long, narrow form of the neolithic barrows of southern England may well prove to be a tribute to that masculine principle. The stones of the avenues leading to Avebury tend to be of two alternating shapes: tall and parallel-sided, representing the male, and short and lozenge-shaped, representing the female (Burl, 1976). It seems more likely that the long and thin shape of the long barrow plan is intended to refer to a male god than to a tall, thin, 'hag' transformation of the goddess, as Michael Dames has asserted (Dames, 1977).

THE LONG BARROWS OF SOUTHERN ENGLAND

In the chalk and clay lands of southern Britain, the building of chambered tombs was not generally practicable. Chalk has a certain strength in resisting erosion *in situ,* in the natural hillside, but when cut it will not bear weight and does not handle well. It has been used very little as a building material, except for some church interiors. On Salisbury Plain, which is a chalk plateau, there is no solid rock suitable for lintels or roof slabs for a chambered tomb or passage-grave. But there are sarsens.

Sarsens are loose boulders, often with exotically gnarled and knobbed surfaces, made of indurated sandstone. They are thought to be the weathered residue of once-continuous layers of Eocene sands, which would originally have capped the chalk rock. The Eocene layers have been almost entirely eroded away to leave just a few remnant slabs of particularly resistant rock. These remnant boulders were common enough on Salisbury Plain for neolithic man to use them as a building material. The great stone circles of Stonehenge and Avebury are made of sarsens: so are the chambers of the West Kennet Long Barrow near Avebury. This remarkable barrow is probably the best preserved in southern England, a complete chambered tomb of the same 'Hyperborean' type found in Orkney. Wayland's Smithy in Berkshire is a similar, trapezoidal chambered barrow, 180 feet long. Most of the other chambered barrows have been eroded down to the rocky tombs, such as Lanyon Quoit in Cornwall, the Spinsters' Rock in Devon and Kit's Coty House in Kent.

Other long barrows in southern England are not chambered but composed of earth and chalk rubble, usually thrown up from the flanking ditches. Along the South Downs, sarsens are rare and generally less than a metre across; chambered barrows of the type found on Salisbury Plain therefore could not be built. There is a clear-cut relationship between geology and barrow type.

In examining the contents of the solid grave-mounds, we come up against one of the recurring problems of the too-accessible hills of the south country. Most of the barrows have been opened, and more than once. The Vikings are often singled out for blame in this respect, and it is known that they entered many neolithic monuments looking for plunder; the Viking runic inscriptions within the great chamber of Maes Howe on Mainland Orkney prove it. Although I hold no brief for Vikings, it must be said that just as much damage was done by the antiquarians of the eighteenth and nineteenth centuries who dug indiscriminately into the barrows on a bizarre range of pretexts. The notorious Dr Troope was gathering human bones for patent remedies; bored gentlemen searched for buried treasure; antiquarians hoped to find artefacts; public-spirited worthies organized the opening of barrows for the entertainment of the lower classes. Some of their finds were recorded: very few were lodged in museums. In terms of modern, systematic archaeology, most of the sites treated in this way were irreparably damaged.

The Revd J. Douglas, who dug up several Sussex barrows in the period 1800-1820, left no adequate record of his deeds. Worse still, he encouraged Dr Gideon Mantell to open barrows in the Lewes area. Mantell, who was a general practitioner in Lewes, became famous after he discovered an iguanodon and other dinosaur remains in the Weald. Like his mentor, Mantell left us little that is of any archaeological value. It is known that he opened the Windover Bowl Barrow in 1833 and found a scraper, some urns and ashes. The opening of Money Burgh shortly afterwards was a more half-hearted affair, undertaken by Joseph Tompsett of Deans, the farm immediately below the barrow. This farmer came across a skeleton not far below the surface. His descendants felt that he had not reached the primary interment so that, although the surface of Money Burgh appears ravaged, it is probable that an untouched burial lies at the heart, or more likely one end, of the mound.

Some long barrows are bound to be empty because they have been gutted by post-neolithic looters. Occasionally, though, it is clear that a long barrow was never used for burial. Again, only occasionally, a long barrow may contain only one burial. Most contain multiple burials of up to fifty individuals. Typically, the long barrow houses the remains of about six people. The corpses are not reverently laid out supine, as in a modern burial, nor are they usually arranged in their crouched position with any sign of care. The skeletons are often found disarticulated and incomplete. At first sight, this appears to be the result of some barbarous rite during which the corpses were torn to pieces and hurled together in a common grave. A more likely scenario is the two-stage funerary rite mentioned earlier. The corpses were first exposed or buried in shallow graves; then, after a year or more, the bones were ready for the second rite — burial in the long barrow.

As six or ten individuals were buried in the long barrow at once, and it is unlikely that this number would die simultaneously, the corpses were presumably allowed to accumulate until the requisite number was reached. Once the right total was reached, or — equally likely in a busy farming community — when time permitted, the bones were gathered up into one place on the chalk turf. Pots were added either as an offering to the Earth Mother or so that the dead had food for the journey to the underworld. Then earth and chalk were dug up from two long trenches and thrown up to form a long mound between the trenches.

THE SUSSEX LONG BARROWS
Altogether, some 230 long barrows have been identified in southern England. There is a marked tendency for them to be concentrated in Wessex and they are nearly all situated on chalk hills. There are only nine authenticated long barrows in Sussex: two in West Sussex and a cluster of seven in East Sussex. The sizes and locations of the Sussex long barrows are as follows:

Barrow	Nearest village	Length	Width (feet)
Bevis's Thumb	Compton	190	65
Long Barrow (Bow Hill)	Stoughton	100	65
Camel's Humps	South Malling	115	65
Money Burgh	Piddinghoe	118	45
Giant's Grave	West Firle	102	65
Long Burgh	Alfriston	180	60
Long Barrow (Fore Down)	Charlston	115	65
Hunter's Burgh	Wilmington	190	75
Windover Long Mound	Wilmington	180	45

The oval barrow near Long Burgh has been omitted because of its uncertain date. Its excavator (Drewett, 1975) confidently assigns it to the neolithic on the basis of a radiocarbon date of 3000 BC from an antler. On the other hand, its oval shape makes it more likely to belong to the transition into the Bronze Age; the burial of a single woman rather than a mass burial tends to support a Bronze Age date, while the leg bones gave a radiocarbon date of only 650 BC. The scatter of neolithic flint flakes in the area might be associated with the indisputably neolithic Long Burgh, just to the south. Long barrows in England generally have a length between one hundred and two hundred feet, and the Sussex barrows conform to this mode.

Of the East Sussex long barrows, only the Giant's Grave on Firle Beacon has even been alleged to possess a chamber. Curwen, writing about the barrow in 1934, felt that the hummocky appearance of the eastern end was consistent with the collapse of an internal timber chamber. There is no excavation evidence for this view. It would nevertheless be quite usual for neolithic builders to have used timber as a substitute for stone, as we shall see later; timber posts were used at Woodhenge to build a circular monument which is thought to have looked similar to Stonehenge, although necessarily a lighter and less durable structure. By pursuing this line of research, we shall again enter the long shadow of the Wilmington Giant, since his 'staves' are in reality enormous baulks of timber (see Chapter 9).

First, some consideration needs to be given to the chronology within which monuments such as the Giant and the long barrows were conceived and created. It is vital to put dates to as many events as possible, in order to avoid inadvertently linking together places and customs that really belong to separate cultures, a mistake that bedevils one occult book after another. A hundred years ago it was all too easy to pile together all the available archaeological evidence and construct from it a romantic picture of druidical empires. Since 1950, the technique of radiocarbon dating has provided fairly accurate dates for organic remains like timber and bone back as far as 50,000 years BP (before present). More recently, tree-rings have been used in order to check radiocarbon dates, especially the annular rings of long-lived species such as the bristlecone pine. Radiocarbon dates are therefore presented in three possible ways: as radiocarbon years BP, as radiocarbon years bc (that is, with the time that has elapsed since the birth of Christ subtracted), or as calendar

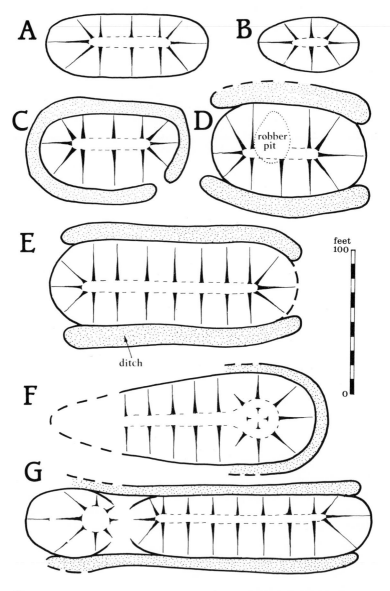

Figure 13. Plans of neolithic long barrows in East Sussex. A: Money Burgh, Piddinghoe. B: Oval Barrow of doubtful age, Alfriston. C: Giant's Grave, Firle Beacon. D: Warrior's Grave, Cliffe Hill. E: Alfriston Long Burgh. F: Hunter's Burgh. G: Windover Long Mound.

years BC. Calendar years are calculated from raw radiocarbon dates, but using the corrections inferred from the bristlecone pine rings.

Some long barrows have been dated by the radiocarbon method, and the period during which they are known to have been constructed stretches from 4200 BC to 2940 BC. This covers the early and middle neolithic and the first part of the late neolithic, which was superseded by the Bronze Age in about 2000 BC. Since relatively few of the long barrows have been assayed by this method, it is safe to assume, pending more dates, that they were built right through the neolithic. Nevertheless, the existing evidence is that they were characteristic of the early and middle neolithic, with the greatest number coming at the close of the early neolithic, 3750-3500 BC.

THE WINDOVER LONG MOUND

Little is known of the rites and practices connected with the preliminary burials; because the structures associated with them were temporary, the archaeological evidence is inevitably slight. Megaw and Simpson (1979) noted that long barrows are sometimes associated with wooden buildings or enclosures that were probably built for preliminary mortuary rites. The buildings or palisaded enclosures were situated at one end of the barrow and were probably used for the temporary burial or exposure of the dead.

On Windover Hill, immediately above the Long Man's left stave, is a narrow artificial terrace, cut about fifteen feet into the hill side. It is situated on the long axis of the Windover Long Mound at its northern end. No purpose has hitherto been suggested for this well-marked terrace, but it is perfectly sited to function as a mortuary enclosure for the dead who were later to be buried in the Long Mound.

The Windover Long Mound is undoubtedly the finest long barrow in Sussex. Approached from the Litlington-Wilmington road along the South Downs Way, it seems to be hiding behind a belt of low bushes in such a way that it becomes fully visible only when the visitor is standing right beside it. The crest of the barrow pitches very slightly towards each end, but its shape creates the overall impression of a smoothly moulded half-cylinder with rounded ends. It does not have the trapezoidal shape of some of the Wessex barrows, but has a constant width of some forty-five feet.

Along each side, the flanking ditches can still be made out, although it can be seen from the comparative lushness of the grass in them that they must be silted up and therefore shallower than when·they were dug. The sides of the mound are perfectly smooth and covered by short downland turf; there is no sign of any disturbance on the surface that might indicate excavation at any time in the past.

One unusual feature of the barrow is its long, thin form. Its length/width ratio is 4.0, as compared with an average of 2.2 for the other Sussex long barrows. This may prove to be significant in the light of another feature peculiar to the barrow, the circular mound that lies on its long axis and is interposed between the northern end of the barrow and the mortuary terrace. Curwen was uncertain whether to treat this as a separate feature or as part of the Long Mound itself. It is very clear, on three separate counts, that the circular mound should be regarded as an integral part of the Long Mound and, moreover, that it was intended from the start to have its present form.

In the first place, the narrow col that joins the circular mound to the Long Mound is at a higher level than the natural level of the hillside immediately to the west; the col has thus been built up and the two mounds are part of a continuous structure. Secondly, the lateral ditches which run along the sides of the Long Mound continue beyond the col to the circular mound. Thirdly, the summit of the smaller mound consists of a circular platform which is at a lower level and is wider than the crest of the Long Mound. The morphology of the two mounds thus implies that they were built conjointly and that their partial separation was a feature of the original design. The probability is that the Long Mound was intended as a phallic symbol. It therefore represents a much larger version of the small fertility talismans found at many neolithic sites.

The significance of this interpretation is twofold. To begin with, it means that the Long Mound is a longer feature than our table of figures suggests: 260 feet long instead of 180. This makes it far and away the longest neolithic cenotaph in Sussex, seventy feet longer than either Hunter's Burgh or Bevis's Thumb. On the basis of its size alone, we are compelled to see this as a site of overriding importance, at least on a regional scale. The extraordinary form of the Long Mound also sets it apart. Although the long, narrow form of the long barrows marks them out as masculine rather than feminine by association, the Windover Long Mound is the only one that is explicitly phallic.

Clearly, this view of the Long Mound identifies the site unambiguously with the fructifying, male sky-god or sun-god, the mysterious consort of the Earth Mother. It gives us the strongest

clue yet to the identity of the colossal figure immediately below it.
As if supporting this identification, the Windover Phallus is
pointing directly towards the Giant's head. The phallic form of the
long barrow is as consistent with neolithic beliefs as the
hemispherical, pregnant-belly form of the passage-grave; both
shapes show a trust that death and burial would result in some kind
of regeneration.

LONG BARROW SITES AND SIGHT-LINES
The Windover Long Mound was built close to the summit of
Windover Hill, and this near-hilltop siting is characteristic of the
East Sussex long barrows in general. The thinking behind this is
worth exploring in some detail, particularly in view of the
proximity of two long barrows to the Long Man.

Neolithic man chose hill tops for burial places for the same
reasons that hill tops and mountain tops have been singled out for
special reverence in nearly every nature-conscious culture.
Tibetans regard the Himalayan peaks as the dwelling places of the
gods. Dante placed his Earthly Paradise at the summit of an immensely high imaginary island in the Southern Ocean, Mount
Purgatory. The Babylonians built a gigantic ziggurat, the
Etemenanki, with a spiral path ascending through seven tiers to a
summit shrine; it was an artificial sacred mountain and came to be
known as the Mount of the Mountains of All Lands. To the people
of Israel it became infamous as the Tower of Babel.

Examples could be multiplied endlessly, but the significance is
clear. For culture after culture, the mountain top is a sacred place. It
gives man a special spiritual exhilaration which is like no other.
There is, built into the collective unconscious, a pattern of deep and
immutable responses that are triggered by primal settings; the sea,
the river, the sky, the cave, the tree and the mountain all produce
deep responses. On a psychological or religious level, it is easy to
see how neolithic ideas of life, death and renewal are dramatized by
hilltop sites. The panoramic vista shows the earth with its
patchwork of lozenge-shaped fields watered by capricious rains,
meadows where cattle may be stranded by unpredictable floods, and
the fragile dwellings of man himself, largely dependent on the
beneficence of the spirit world. Directly below is the underworld,
the Earth Mother, to which all must return for regeneration.
Above is the weather-dictating, season-governing sky. The hilltops
could have been seen as the interface between the three realms, one

inhabited by man and the other two ruled by elemental deities, the earth-goddess and the sky-god.*

The long barrow closest to the Wilmington Giant, the Windover Long Mound, is only 300 feet away from the summit of Windover Hill and stands at 590 feet above sea level. From the Long Mound there are extensive views in all directions except to the south-east, the direction of the summit itself. It is possible to see the sites of the neighbouring long barrows of Hunter's Burgh, half a mile away to the north-east, and Long Burgh, two miles due west. Further away still is the summit of Firle Beacon with its Giant's Grave.

The axis of the Long Mound is oriented north-east to south-west, while that of Hunter's Burgh is oriented north-north-west to south-south-west; there seems to be no significance at all in the orientation of the barrows. Like the Long Mound, Hunter's Burgh is sited just off the summit, this time of Wilmington Hill; it stands on the north-east slope at about 615 feet above sea level. From Hunter's Burgh, the view is materially the same as that from the Long Mound, but something else is visible too. One and three-quarter miles away to the south-east, on the far side of the Jevington wind gap, is another hilltop feature, one of the rare proven settlement sites of neolithic Sussex, the Combe Hill causewayed enclosure.

From the Giant's Grave on Firle Beacon there is a superb view to the north-west, west, south-west and south. The Grave is on the western shoulder of Firle Beacon at 700 feet and from it one can see the Mount Caburn massif, with the Camel's Humps just hidden from view behind the summit of Cliffe Hill at 520 feet. To the south-west, the site of Money Burgh in the Ouse valley is visible, though not easy to pick out. On the horizon to the west-south-west, it is usually possible to make out the grandstand on Brighton Race Course, nearly ten miles away. At the same height, three hundred yards to the south of the grandstand, is a badly damaged neolithic earthwork. This is Whitehawk, another settlement site of the same type as Combe Hill. Excavations there have revealed details of neolithic ritual structures that will give us important evidence concerning the significance of the Long Man's staves.

---

*Sky-orientation is very evident at sites such as Stonehenge, whose stones have been proved to relate closely to the movements of the sun and moon. The archaeological evidence for the worship of the sky-god will be discussed in Chapters 9 and 12.

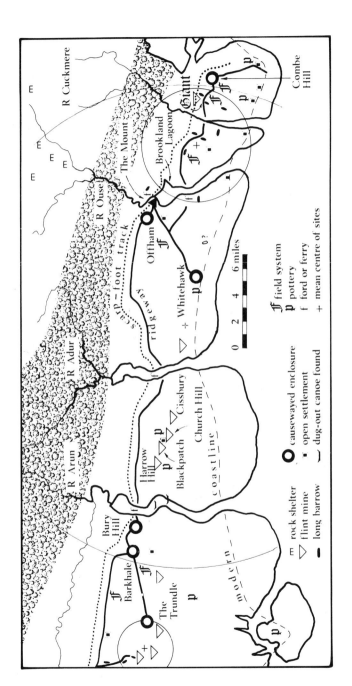

Figure 14. Map of neolithic Sussex. Some of the ancient field systems probably date back to the neolithic. The rock shelters out in the Weald were used as seasonal hunting lodges. For an explanation of mean centres, see Appendix I.

The settlement sites are obviously crucial to any understanding of the movements and practices of the neolithic people of the area and the relationship between the two camps, the barrows and the Long Man will be examined in the next chapter.

Two of the long barrows in the East Sussex group are anomalous; they are neither on nor close to hilltops and the views they command are consequently less extensive. One of these is Money Burgh, which stands on the western side of the Ouse valley only 120 feet above sea level. From the A275, which runs directly below it, the long barrow is quite hard to spot except in an evening light. The area is not rich in neolithic remains, so the general location is distinctly odd. But when I sat on it and looked round, I was surprised how extensive a view it commanded. The Camel's Humps are visible on the skyline to the north, and the Priory Mount in Lewes is just visible to the north-north-west (see Chapter 10); if the next spur to the north jutted out only another hundred yards into the valley, that sight-line would be destroyed. More significant still, the Giant's Grave on Firle Beacon is just visible in a narrow col between Beddingham Hill and Fore Hill. From the road on the valley floor, only 120 feet lower, Firle Beacon cannot be seen.

What emerges is that the long barrows have been very carefully sited close to the summits of high hills, with the exception of Money Burgh and Charlston Long Barrow, which need to be discussed separately. A major consideration in the choice of site has evidently been the extent of the view, which is in every case aesthetically superb. In particular, the surveyors or surveyor-priests have chosen sites that give significant intervisibility with other major neolithic sites in the area, especially other long barrows or camps.

It almost looks as if the monumental landscape was laid out according to some geometrical method by the surveyor-priests. Whether the invisible network of sight-lines can be explained in purely mechanical or pragmatic terms is open to discussion: it seems unlikely. Certainly it would make no sense to impose a layout of anachronistic pentacles or magic squares on the intervisibility lines. It may be possible to make sense of them in terms of what has come to be called 'astral power'. The long barrows and causewayed enclosures were seen as sacred sites; if each one was a gathering place for the regenerative force, it follows logically that each one will also have been regarded as a point from which that force was transmitted. The intervisibility lines may thus have been seen as airways along which the power for renewal might pass to and fro, enhancing the sanctity of all the sites.

The site of the Charlston Long Barrow is difficult to interpret in this context. It is situated on the south-facing slope of a secluded downland valley, Charlston Bottom. Since it stands at only 210 feet and the valley sides rise to twice that height, the view from this site is much more restricted than at any of the other barrow sites. The view to the west takes in Hindover Hill, where an apparently round barrow is hemmed in between the road from Seaford to Alfriston and a precipitous river cliff. The western end of this barrow has been damaged by the convergence of tracks and roads over many centuries, and the possibility of a lost long barrow site can be floated. In that case, the position of the Charlston Long Barrow can be understood rather better. It is visible from the Hindover site, which in turn is visible from Windover Hill.

Curwen, writing in 1934, was uncertain whether the Charlston barrow was a long barrow at all. In a way, it would be easier to agree with his doubt and remove Charlston from the list of Sussex long barrows. It would save us the difficulty and embarrassment of trying to explain its inconsistent position in relation to the known long barrows, none of which sight onto it. But that will not do. I visited the site recently and found it in a sorry state. It has been levelled by treasure-hunters and is now covered with a dense thicket of gorse and thorns. The farmer conscientiously ploughs round the site, so at least the thicket is left as a marker. I was lucky enough to find a small worked flint next to the barrow site. It was a neolithic scraper, which tends to support the view that the barrow too is neolithic.

PEOPLE OF THE BARROWS
Neolithic society is generally agreed to have been more egalitarian than any subsequent community living in southern England. The absence of precious grave-goods or any indication of rank in the burials so far discovered from this era tend to support the idea of an unstratified society.

Yet there is a problem when the number of long barrow burials is added up. If there are 230 long barrows in Wessex, each containing the bones of ten or twenty people, then the barrows account for only 2000-5000 people dying throughout the whole region. This would be a very low total indeed, even if the barrows represented a period of 1300 years, the minimum period spanned by the radiocarbon dates. The population of Wessex is estimated to have been between 10,000 and 30,000 (Burl, 1976; Renfrew, 1974). Since only two or three people per year were being treated to burial in a long barrow across the whole region, it is clear that only a tiny proportion of the population — perhaps between 1 and 5 per cent — were privileged in this way.

This implies that neolithic society was, after all, stratified in some way. If preferential treatment was intended, it would be useful to know who the privileged few were. A first thought is that the long barrow people were kinglets or chieftains and their wives and offspring (Megaw and Simpson, 1979), but there are no grave-goods that might verify this. It is equally possible that the privileged group consisted of priests or shamans, the instinctual holy men who steered the community through the repeating crises of seasonal changes by making rain, abating floods, willing the start of summer and calling the wild boar. Or they may have been the surveyors and astronomers, who watched the sky and the calendar; such men were vital to the efficient organization of the farming year, and their special gifts would have been likely to bring them special honours.

There is another explanation entirely, though, and it is one that suits the archaeological evidence better than any notion of a social élite. In spite of the monumental impressiveness of the barrows, the local details of each of the interments show them to have been in- dividually unceremonious: indeed, as unceremonious as the apparently secular burials discovered at Whitehawk, which will be discussed in the next chapter. It seems rather as if a few token corpses were offered — perhaps taken at random or selected by augury — as a validation of the barrow. The barrow was evidently not intended specifically as a memorial to the people who were buried inside it. The long barrows — particularly the most elaborate ones — have a size and structure at variance with the casualness of the individual interments.

It is more appropriate to regard the long barrows as sacred cenotaphs, as monuments, not to the dead, but to Death itself. The barrows are gateways to eternity, through which the magic cycle of birth, growth, death and rebirth may be generated anew. These important concepts were doubtless celebrated with elaborate ceremony, in story, song and prayer, even though small honour was accorded to the bones of the individual people chosen to validate the monuments. The burials were necessary to authenticate the cenotaphs, nonetheless, as an earnest of the builders' seriousness and commitment to the great and magical enterprise: a recognition of their place in the web of earthbound life.

In mythological terms, the long barrows represent the nadir of man's path through the cycle; they are a plangent acknowledgement of the lowest point, the vanishing of man into earth. Yet they also represent the hope of re-emergence and renewal. They contain the two diametrically opposite emotional stresses of despair and hope, of dying and being born, of sadness and joy. It is here, perhaps unexpectedly, that we stumble once more on the Long Man. So far we have caught occasional glimpses of his identity, fleetingly and in the far distance. Now, suddenly, we are much closer to the heart of the mystery than ever before, even if the long barrows may seem at first sight far removed from the matter of the Long Man.

Like the passing seasons, like the moon and the sun, like man himself, the Giant rises from obscurity, has his hour of glory and then subsides into oblivion once more. The Giant will emerge as an heroic figure, powerful and commanding enough to superintend the generation of man, his animals and his crops; and yet, in some mysterious way, he is ready to surrender a part of that immense power in order to participate in the strange, periodic dance of life and death.

9. GATEWAYS FOR THE GOD

Through the unknown remembered gate
When the last of earth left to discover
Is that which was the beginning.

T. S. Eliot, *Little Gidding.*

SUSSEX FLINT MINES

High in the rural downland of West Sussex, traces of the oldest industry in the kingdom still survive. On the summit of Church Hill, just to the west of Findon village, a hummocky surface marks the sites of several vertical shafts that led down to the rich seams of flint below. Once the miners reached the seams, they followed them laterally for a short distance along galleries leading radially away from the access shafts. After the archaeologists had explored them, the shafts were filled in again for safety.

The Church Hill mines yielded antler-picks that were used for a radiocarbon assay, and the date showed that the flint mines were being worked as early as 3390 bc (4200 BC). The neighbouring hill tops were also the scene of early mining. Cissbury, a mile away to the east on the far side of the Findon valley, had a cluster of flint mines, though the site is now dominated by the great Iron Age fortress that caps the hill. A mile to the north-west is Blackpatch Hill, whose miners left behind antler-picks which have been dated to 4000 BC.

The availability of flints was crucial to the neolithic way of life.

Apart from farm produce, flints were the key commodity in the economy. They were skilfully broken and chipped into a variety of shapes to make hammers, knives, daggers, axes, spear-heads, arrow-heads and scrapers: in other words, to make most of the weapons and tools that were needed. Since this central section of the South Downs was the location of the earliest known neolithic flint mines in the country, it might be expected to have had early commercial and social links with the acknowledged heartland of the Wessex culture on Salisbury Plain. Yet, if there were early contacts between the two areas, their evolution later diverged. Either way, the significant feature is the very early date at which the neolithic culture took off in the South Downs. The development of that culture is more difficult to date, since the long barrows could have been built at any time during the early or middle neolithic. The presence of causewayed enclosures and the absence of henges tends to reinforce the evidence of the flint mines — that the neolithic remains of Sussex are early rather than late. But that inference may well prove to be too facile, and it is quite possible that the 'early' design of the causewayed camps was in use right through the neolithic.

THE CAUSEWAYED ENCLOSURES
The Combe Hill camp stands on a commanding 620 foot summit, with the main chalk escarpment falling precipitously to the north and east. The camp follows the usual pattern of causewayed camps, with a hilltop site, oval plan and concentric but discontinuous ditches. Inside each ditch is a bank, also discontinuous, so that the central space has many access causeways. The causewayed camps show no sign of permanent settlement; there are no traces of buildings or pit dwellings in or near them. There is, on the other hand, plenty of evidence of temporary occupation, which is thought to have been seasonal. In southern England as a whole about forty such enclosures have been discovered so far.

In terms of date, they rank with the earliest neolithic innovations, giving dates from 4300 to 3250 BC. The Windmill Hill causewayed enclosure, which is close beside Avebury and thought to be Avebury's precursor, is the most celebrated of the seasonal settlements. The ditches at Windmill Hill were filled with domestic refuse and this gives an indication of the approximate proportions of the livestock kept there: 66 per cent cattle, 16 per cent pigs and 12 per cent sheep.

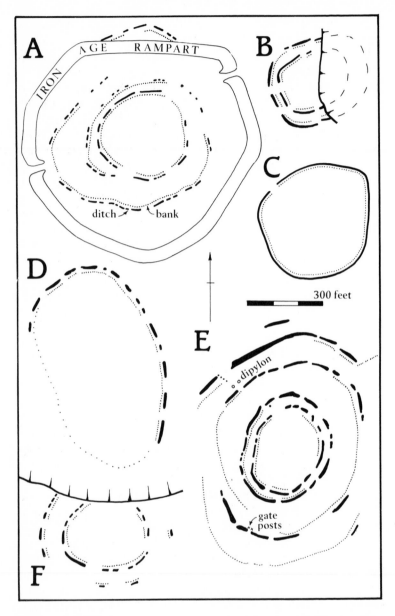

Figure 15. Plans of Sussex causewayed enclosures. A: The Trundle (3750 BC). B: Offham Hill. C: Bury Hill (3500 BC). D: Barkhalc. E: Combe Hill. F: Whitehawk.

The overall size of the Whitehawk causewayed enclosure at Brighton, with its long axis at 900 feet, is exactly twice that of Combe Hill. Whitehawk is nevertheless small by comparison with the sites on Salisbury Plain: 10 acres compared with 21 at Windmill Hill, 29 at Avebury and 34 at Marden. Whitehawk has four concentric oval ditches compared with only two at Combe Hill. It stands on a spur at about 360 feet, in a shallow saddle between two hills. Like Combe Hill, its site is flanked on two sides by very steep slopes, to the west into Baker's Bottom and to the east into Whitehawk Bottom.

In spite of the differences detectable between one neolithic enclosure and the next, one feature remains surprisingly constant. If the long axes of the innermost oval enclosures are measured, their dimensions are found to be strikingly similar. The Trundle is 350 feet, Avebury South Circle 330 feet, Avebury North Circle 310 feet, Combe Hill, Whitehawk, Windmill Hill and Stonehenge I all 300 feet. Their common size suggests at least an initial common purpose.

What that purpose was is still a matter for debate. Some archaeologists think that the causewayed enclosures were market centres. Others believe that they were settlements, ceremonial centres or even graveyards where corpses were exposed as a preliminary to burial in the long barrow. One of the most enigmatic examples is the now-destroyed enclosure on Offham Hill, north of Lewes. Offham Hill is lower than Combe Hill, at about 400 feet, but it commands a view that is every bit as impressive. From the crest fifty feet south of the enclosure, the modern panorama clears the two patches of woodland that embower the ravaged neolithic site; from this viewpoint there are unobstructed sight-lines north across the Wealden vale, east across the Ouse valley towards the Warrior's Grave, Mount Caburn and Firle Beacon, and south-west into the Brookland basin. The site chosen for Offham illustrates once again how important the aesthetic criterion was to neolithic man.

Like Combe Hill, Offham had two concentric ditched banks surrounding an oval enclosure that may originally have been some 290 feet long. When the site was totally excavated in 1976, it had already been reduced to a 'D' shape by chalk quarrying.

The enigma of Offham resides in the sheer poverty of the site. An unusually thorough rescue dig yielded disappointingly little. The crouch burial of an adult was found in one of the ditches, together with a few sherds of pottery of the same type as that found at Whitehawk. There was just one hint of contact with the outside world: a single chip of Cornish granite (Drewett, 1977).

The apparently very low level of neolithic activity at Offham as compared with Whitehawk may be explained in terms of some advantage, whether economic or magical, real or imagined, that neolithic man attributed to Whitehawk. Whitehawk, in other words, sapped Offham's vitality. An alternative possibility is that Offham was designed as a centre for religious ceremonies but that a site nearby superseded it once its inherent sanctity had been recognized. There is good reason to suppose that the new, ascendant sacred site was in Lewes — not two miles from Offham (see Chapters 10 and 11).

The ditches at Whitehawk were explored in several excavations in the 1930s and were found to contain a large volume of neolithic debris. The ditches were not required for defence, or they would not have been filled in this way. Amongst the rubbish were potsherds from vessels up to ten inches in diameter. None of the pots had flat bases: instead they had lugs or perforations through which cords were threaded for carrying. The design is consistent with people coming in from the surrounding farmland armed with their own supplies of water, broth and possibly alcohol.

The Whitehawk ditches also contain flint arrow-heads, axe-heads and scrapers. A small number of artefacts made of chalk created problems of interpretation when they were found, and those problems have still to be resolved. A small, four-sided chalk tablet, four inches square and marked with a curious criss-cross pattern is particularly puzzling. The purpose of the so-called 'chessboard' seems almost to be beyond guessing. Is it a game, a map, or possibly a hieroglyph? Since the lozenge shape that occurs in many other neolithic drawings is thought to represent the sown field (Gimbutas, 1974), the 'chessboard' could represent an idealized map or ideograph of a field system. As such, it might have been used in a fertility ritual or carried as a fertility talisman.

More intriguing still is the similarity it bears to the pattern of ardmarks discovered beneath the neolithic long barrow at South Street in Wiltshire. The criss-cross pattern of early ploughing, dating from 3600 BC or earlier, is associated with the preparation of the soil for sowing cereals: so perhaps the talisman carries some such meaning as 'We have ploughed the soil and made it ready; now it is for you to cause the barley to ripen', a reminder to the sky-

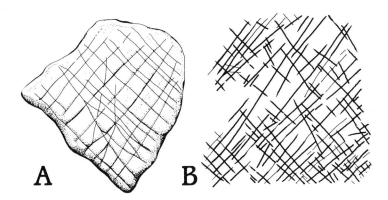

Figure 16. A neolithic fertility talisman. The 'Chessboard' (A) is a chalk tablet found at the Whitehawk causewayed enclosure. The criss-cross pattern is similar to that of the ard-marks (B) found under the South Street long barrow in Wiltshire.

god of his part in the communal effort, a kind of prayer. Or perhaps, more simply, it is an early version of 'Kilroy was here' — 'We are the people who plough'.

Another chalk tablet found in the Trundle causewayed enclosure is carved with sub-parallel, confluent and diffluent waving lines. This obvious water symbol may have been intended to represent streaming rain, if the lines are read as vertical, or a flood or the sea, if they are read as horizontal. Either way, it makes sense interpreted as a fertility ideograph relating back to the all-important harvest.

Some rounded and perforated objects found at Whitehawk have been interpreted as loom-weights. It is hard to visualize people travelling to a temporary fair, livestock market or religious feast carrying looms. We can believe either that the objects had some other function, such as weights for fishing nets, or that the people were more sedentary. Indeed, it is now being suggested that this enclosure, along with others of its type, was permanently settled; the small, lightweight, wooden shelters would leave few if any archaeological traces and could easily be missed in a partial excavation. A compromise interpretation is probably more satisfactory still. The causewayed enclosure may have been inhabited all the year round by a small nucleus of people, a single, 'caretaker' clan, which acted as host to the clans of surrounding areas on feast days.

The precise purpose of the intermittent gatherings at Whitehawk is not known for certain. It is thought that they were multi-purpose, serving as important social occasions for an otherwise scattered rural community — as livestock markets, as fairs, as moots, as occasions for religious ceremonies. The large amount of domestic rubbish filling the ditches is typical of causewayed enclosures generally and, indeed, of the great wooden henge monuments of the Wessex heartland. Evan Hadingham (1975) notes that at Durrington Walls fragments of individual pots have been found strewn all over the enclosure, suggesting a level of activity well beyond normal carelessness. The remarkable distribution of the debris can best be explained in terms of wild and riotous feasting. During the revels, pots and cups were hurled about and quite deliberately smashed; food too was thrown around with wild abandon, even across the entrance causeways.

The concentric barriers between the causeways are perhaps best seen in ritual terms rather than practical terms, although it is possible to see a use for them. They may have been used to control and segregate animals of different types; with simple hurdles made of chestnut or hazel, it would have been easy to close off one or all of the outer enclosures. Additional hurdles could have been used radially to divide the baileys into pens. The visitors brought oxen, pigs, goats, sheep and dogs as their domestic animals and may well have needed to pen them in some way. An autumn moot could have been used to slaughter surplus livestock before the onset of winter; the feasting might be seen as a response to the unusual meat glut in the first instance, but the hunted carcases of red deer, roe deer and wild boar were taken into the enclosure as well.

The concentric design of the enclosures certainly had a symbolic, ritual value. It is reminiscent of the concentric 'cup-and-ring' rock carvings of the Highlands, the stone circles and the ubiquitous neolithic spirals. A sun symbol seems the obvious interpretation, but the more complex connotations of the spiral are better left for a later discussion (see Chapter 10). The repetition of the concentric circle design confirms that it was another ideograph, like the markings on the chalk tablets, but one which was felt to be of such overriding importance that it had to be drawn large enough to contain the entire community. What idea, what natural phenomenon was of such overriding importance? What else but the sun? Perhaps a later analogue for the neolithic farmers and their relationship with their sun symbol is the medieval magician withdrawing into the safety and security of his carefully drawn pentacle, comfortable in the knowledge that hostile powers could never enter.

In fact, magicians of many periods have withdrawn into the safety of a circle instead of a pentacle. The *Key of Solomon*, mentioned in Chapter 3 as the most notorious grimoire of the Middle Ages, gives details of several magical rituals but insists that no activity involving contact with the spirit world can succeed without the drawing and consecration of a magic circle. The *Key* gives an account of the elaborate ceremonies of purification and dedication which must precede the drawing of the circle, together with a discussion of the site: a ruined building or a graveyard is suitable.

The circle is inscribed on the earth with the Knife of the Art and a rope nine feet long. After this, a second circle with a radius of eight feet is marked, concentric with the first. Here there is a distant parallel with the patterns of the causewayed enclosures and henges of neolithic England. They are all made up of double concentric circles: units of bank-and-ditch or ditch-and-bank. The gap between the medieval earth-inscribed circles was used for writing the Names of Power, but that is probably a late addition to the exercise.

For certain rituals, a cluster of satellite circles or an overlay of pentacles may be necessary. When these are ready, only a small entrance gap is left in the magic circle. The magician enters. If he has disciples he ushers them into the protection of the sacred precinct and closes the circle. Then, safe in their refuge, the invocants may begin the rites of consecration and conjuration.

The magician falls to his knees and recites the consecration of the circle:

'O Earth! I conjure thee, by the holiest name ASHER EHEIEH, with this arc made by my own hand! May God bless this place with all the heavenly virtues. May no defiling spirit be able to enter this Circle or cause discomfort to anyone within it. O Lord God! I beg thee to bless this Circle, and this whole place and all of us herein. Give us safety as thou art the Everlasting Ruler!'

The formal conjuration and dismissal of spirits follows.

This is only one form which the magic circle and its rite took. In some cults it shrank to a metal ring, which of itself conjured genii, whilst in others, especially in the late Middle Ages, magicians prudently carried folding paper circles: in Babylon, sorcerers used a ring of flour. Nevertheless, the underlying principles seem to remain fairly constant. A liturgy for the consecration of the Circle of Protection has been found scratched on ancient Sumerian clay tablets, dating from 2000 BC. Thus a continuous tradition of magic circle beliefs and rituals can be traced very nearly back to the time of the English neolithic earth-circles, and certainly to the fullest development of Stonehenge.

Figure 17.   The magic circle. The magician is safe from the powers of evil inside his magic circle (from a sixteenth-century woodcut).

The sun-symbol plans of Combe Hill, Offham and Whitehawk are also a reminder that neolithic man was not solely preoccupied with Earth Mother worship, but recognized the power of the sun-god as well. There is another reminder of the sun-god at White-hawk, but it is by no means immediately obvious; the link is a pathetic and rather unpromising child-burial.

Of the three crouch burials discovered at Whitehawk, the first was the skeleton of a middle-aged man. The second was the burial of a woman with a newborn child. Hadingham takes this as evidence that the neolithic was a harsh and violent period, which is an exaggerated view. English women died in childbirth very commonly, even in the well-nourished middle classes, as recently as the nineteenth century: few would describe the Victorian bourgeoise as suffering violence and hardship. Neither should the apparent casualness of the burials disconcert us. Neolithic death rites simply did not involve the Christian practice of careful laying-out; it was not considered important which way a corpse's limbs rested. Whether the crouch was used because it required a smaller hole, and therefore less work, or because it resembled the yet-unborn child, is impossible to say. Conversely, a recognizable, modern concern for the dead is shown by the touching grave-gift of fossil sea-urchins buried with the Whitehawk woman.

The third burial, that of a seven-year-old child, was found in a deep pit between the third and fourth ditches in the north-west quadrant of the enclosure. Shallow graves were the norm, so the depth of this grave is unusual. The child was found in a hole thirty inches in diameter drilled seven feet below the present land surface. The shape of the hole, with its relatively narrow bore and vertical sides is consistent with a setting for a monoxyl or wooden pylon. There are many small post-holes along the crests of the banks, designed to support a light palisade, but the deep hole is obviously a setting for a very tall baulk of timber. The narrow trench excavated in the 1930s missed the second pylon setting, which may lie thirty feet to the north-east or north-west.

THE DIPYLON GATES AND THE MIDSUMMER SUN-GOD

The two tall posts at Whitehawk served as ceremonial gate posts. An earlier excavation by Curwen revealed another smaller dipylon gate to the south, immediately inside a gap in the third ditch. This second gate lies exactly on the enclosure's long axis and may represent one of its main entrances. The post-holes of the second gate were 1 foot in diameter, 3 feet deep and 7 feet apart. So far, no other causewayed enclosures have been found with such substantial post-holes (Megaw and Simpson, 1979). No-one has linked the tall wooden masts with the Long Man's staves but the connection, once seen, is so obvious that it scarcely needs elaboration. The putative ceremonial pylons, the *non*-functional gateway, rising thirty or forty feet above the low earth banks and palisades of the enclosure must have made a striking landmark, especially since the site occupies a dramatic skyline position that can be seen from Combe Hill and Windover.

There are no other clues from Whitehawk concerning the pylons' significance; so, before we can finally identify the god-like figure standing at the dipylon gate, a wider search for similar gates elsewhere must be made. The obvious starting point is that 'Dance of the Giants' — Stonehenge itself.

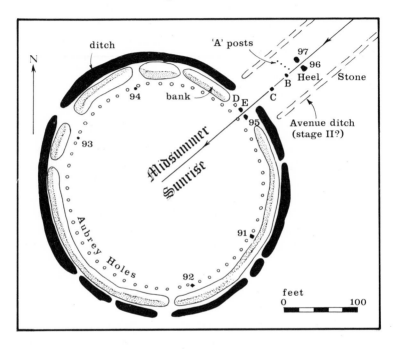

Figure 18.   Plan of Stonehenge I, 2900-2400 BC. The recent discovery of a stone-hole (here called 97) next to the Heel Stone explains why the latter does not align accurately on the pre-2000 BC midsummer sunrise. The first flash of the neolithic sunrise passed between the two stones.

Stonehenge has had so much written about it that we could easily lose ourselves in a welter of detail that may be fascinating but that sheds no light on the Long Man mystery. It is important, though, to remember that Stonehenge was a long time a-building — a thousand years — and that the concepts of the designers evidently changed significantly between and during the phases of building. One thing remained consistent, and that was the formality of the site's function through the various structural phases; there is no trace of the domestic litter that is found at occupation sites such as

Whitehawk and Durrington Walls. We must also bear in mind the impressive technology that was applied to this site, an indication of its vast importance. The Great Pyramid of Cheops is often spoken of with awe, but the largest individual stone in it weighs only fifteen tons; the largest stone at Stonehenge, Stone 56, is estimated to weigh fifty tons.

The first phase in the building of Stonehenge, usually referred to as Stonehenge I, began in about 2180 bc (2900 BC). It was a relatively simple monument consisting of a circular ditch enclosing a circular bank 320 feet in diameter, 20 feet wide and 7 feet high. Immediately inside the bank a ring of 56 pits was dug, each containing cremated bones and other offerings. The centre of the henge remained empty as far as can be judged from solid archaeological evidence, but it is thought that some post-holes may indicate a light wooden structure of some kind.

Just outside the henge stood the Heel Stone; a straight line from the centre of the concentric circles to the point of the leaning Heel Stone is oriented to the place on the horizon where the sun rises on the summer solstice. This is the best-known of several astronomical alignments at Stonehenge. Along this sight-line there is a gap in the bank and ditch marking an important ceremonial entrance to the henge. That entrance was marked by two portal stones, one of which survives as the so-called Slaughter Stone. Although now fallen, it still gives us an idea of its original appearance, with its length of 22 feet.

The fact that the Heel Stone leans in towards the sight-line passing between the portal stones has puzzled many observers. Surely, they argue, if neolithic man had wanted a fore-sight at that point, he possessed the skill to erect the stone vertically in the right place? It would, for one thing, have been more stable if vertical; like the other stones of the monument, the Heel Stone is only balanced in a shallow socket: it is not deeply buried. The original engineers, who poised their stones with great care, would have known that a leaning stone would, in a matter of centuries, become a fallen stone. If, as some think, the Heel Stone has overbalanced or been pushed into its present position, the key orientation of Stonehenge, the sight-line on the midsummer sunrise, does not exist except as a chance occurrence. Or does it? Excavations in 1980-81 revealed that beside the Heel Stone there once stood another stone. The newly discovered socket of this lost stone shows that the Heel Stone and its partner originally formed a second, outer pair of portal stones.

In the simplest and oldest design of Stonehenge there were only four large menhirs on the site: the 16 feet high Heel Stones, which heralded and celebrated the arrival of the summer solstice, and the two inner portal stones, which probably stood about 19 feet high at the entrance to the henge. The pairs of portal stones were clearly of profound ritual significance, although we can now only speculate as to their precise function.

Yet perhaps the answer is the obvious one. Stonehenge I was designed to pinpoint the midsummer sunrise as the pivotal event of the calendar. As its builders were the earliest farmers, their dependence on the sun's strength in high summer was absolute. Since it is known from other remains that they did not distinguish between ecological and spiritual relationships, it can be assumed that the appearance of the midsummer sun — in its full power in the astronomical and ecological senses — would be seen as the most complete manifestation of the sun-god. The passage of the sun's rays between the Heel Stones and the inner portals to the henge-centre would have been treated as a visitation of the greatest importance. The portals were thus the doorway through which the sun-god passed in his annual journey from the mazey sky to the world of men. The broken magic circle, remember, allows the chief sorcerer to enter with his disciples; perhaps the sun-god himself was regarded as the magician.

Lesser features of Stonehenge I were the four small Station Stones set in the circle of Aubrey Holes. These acted as multiple markers for the sunset and moonset at the winter solstice as well as moonrise and sunrise at the summer solstice.

Stonehenge II was an experimental phase, which was fairly quickly abandoned in favour of a design that was both more ambitious and more primitive. Starting in about 2100 BC and ending in about 2050 BC, the centre of the henge was developed with two circles of bluestones. The portals were removed and re-erected radially nearer to the Heel Stone. They were still aligned with the midsummer sunrise but no longer regarded as a symbolic doorway. Significantly, this phase lasted only fifty years and the bluestone circles were never completed. The bluestones were rooted out in a major change of plan and replaced in Stonehenge III by the magnificent sarsen circle and the horseshoe of sarsen trilithons. Some one-and-a-half million man-days of hard work were invested in this stage of Stonehenge's evolution. More significantly still, for this zenith phase, the portal stones were reinstated in their original positions.

Thus, both in the opening phase of Stonehenge's history, from 2900 BC to 2100 BC, and in the culminating phase beginning in 1800 BC and continuing into the Bronze Age, the principal alignment of the monument was celebrated by a pair of mast-like stones forming a ritual doorway for the sun-god. At what stage the Heel Stone's missing companion was removed may never be known, but the significance of the sight-line is undiminished whether it was marked by four or by two portal stones.

Not far from Stonehenge is the settlement which Aubrey Burl (1976) believes housed the community which built the great astronomical temple. Durrington Walls is only two miles away to the east and it appears to have been predominantly secular in function, although the same grooved pottery has been unearthed at both sites, showing that the same people used both sites. Durrington Walls is surrounded by an earth bank and ditch, but no attempt was made by its builders to approximate a circle. The huge enclosure, 1600 feet across and covering over 30 acres, is estimated to have taken nearly a million man-hours to build, largely because of the extraordinary wooden rotundas that were erected inside it. Three radiocarbon dates show that the site was being developed from 2500 BC onwards and was still in use 250 years later.

Figure 19. Durrington Walls. A reconstruction of the great Southern Rotunda, showing the massive dipylon gate which faced the midwinter sunrise, *c.*2500 BC.

Durrington Walls has two main entrances, one to the north-west, the other to the south-east. The larger of the two wooden rotundas stood immediately inside the south-east entrance with its doorway also open to the south-east. Again there is confirmation that neolithic man was building in a period of peace and confidence; there is no sign of military defence here at all. The two rotundas were discovered during a dig at Durrington Walls that was fairly restricted in area. It is quite possible that even more spectacular monuments are awaiting discovery in the unexcavated western half of the large enclosure.

The larger rotunda has been reconstructed by archaeologists from the maze of post-holes on the site of the structure. The building was circular, 127 feet in diameter and covered by a pitched conical roof. The central courtyard was left open to the sky. But the entrance is the most telling part of the reconstruction. Two massive post-holes show that two pylons, taller than any of the pillars supporting the roof, marked the ceremonial doorway. Once again, as at Stonehenge and Whitehawk, the doorway is marked out as especially symbolic. The Durrington Walls door-posts are estimated to have been three feet in diameter, sixteen feet apart and over thirty-two feet high.

It is clear from this small sample of neolithic religious and occupation sites that the dipylon gate had a powerful significance to neolithic man. Unfortunately, the archaeological evidence tells us only implicitly of the great height of the masts; exact figures would be preferable. Inevitably, no wooden pylon has survived and the taller stone monoliths have fallen and disintegrated. One thinks immediately of the Grand Menhir Brisé, a great stone monolith which now lies fallen and shattered in Brittany. It would have been 70 feet long when intact and therefore stood 60 feet tall when planted vertically. The Grand Menhir weighed 340 tons and lighter wooden monoxyls were easy to erect by comparison. The Durrington Walls South Rotunda's door-posts were held by post-holes seven feet deep and therefore could have risen to a height of forty feet.

At Maumbury Rings, near Dorchester, there is a circle of forty-four shafts dug up to thirty-five feet down into the chalk. Hadingham declares that they were obviously not intended as settings for timber posts, yet it seems the only rational inter-pretation. Their incredible depth simply shows that the monoxyls they were designed to hold secure were immensely tall: a hundred feet is not inconceivable. Although Durrington Walls, Mount Pleasant and Woodhenge were probably all designed as roofed rotundas, not all the wooden structures were covered. The eight massive post-holes arranged in a horseshoe at Arminghall in Norfolk are spaced too far apart to have supported a roof. So, at that site, dated 3400 BC, eight tall and separate monumental timbers reared skywards like totem poles.

Twin poles are sometimes associated with long barrows. The 'total' excavation of Wor Barrow at Handley in Dorset by General Pitt-Rivers in 1894 has left the site an absolute wreck. It did at least uncover a wooden mortuary enclosure measuring 90 feet by 35. In it were planted two large posts with three male burials between them; the bodies had been covered first by a temporary turf 'house' and then by the long barrow itself. This is a rare association between the life-giving masts of the sun-god and death, but the seasonal vegetal cycle is a tightly knit system, both naturally and mythogenically, with birth and death, growth and decay, seedtime and harvest, winter and summer, youth and age indissolubly linked. Each thing grows out of its opposite.

If the Long Man's staves represent a neolithic dipylon gate, we are well on the way to deciphering the central religious significance of the Long Man picture, as well as identifying the Long Man himself. But first we need to look at the more concrete aspect of the mystery. If the staves are a ceremonial gate, are they a representation of gates in general, as a common feature of neolithic sites, or are they a representation of a particular gate? If specific pylons are shown, it is probable that a local site is indicated, if only because we know that the ceremonial portals were widespread. Whitehawk is more likely as the subject of the carving than Stonehenge or Durrington Walls. The Combe Hill causewayed enclosure is closer still to the Wilmington Giant, and excavation on that site may eventually reveal similar masts. They have certainly not been discovered so far.

Incredibly, only a few square feet of the Combe Hill site have been excavated, by Reginald Musson in 1949. The people who used Combe Hill in the neolithic were using a type of pottery which is rare in Wessex and Sussex and is not found in any other causewayed enclosure, except for a very small amount at Whitehawk. The 'Ebbsfleet' pottery is regarded as the earliest type of 'Peterborough' style pottery, which belongs to the middle and late neolithic. Ebbsfleet ware characteristically has impressions of twisted cord and fingernails to create simple patterns. It dates to about 2100-2700 BC and it means that Combe Hill was occupied at the time when Stonehenge I, Durrington Walls and Avebury were being built. When Musson found this relatively late ware in 1950, he was amazed that late neolithic folk were still using a causewayed enclosure.

This underlines an important difference between the East Sussex culture and the 'mainstream' culture of Salisbury Plain. The cause-wayed camp was regarded as inadequate in the heartland and the henge was developed as a replacement. In East Sussex, the cause-wayed camp continued in use and there is no sign of a henge ever having been attempted. There are even significant differences between the potsherds at Whitehawk and those at Combe Hill. Whitehawk yielded a mass of fragments belonging to the Windmill Hill type, but very little Ebbsfleet ware, whilst Combe Hill was exclusively Ebbsfleet. So, in addition to the obvious divergences from Wessex, Combe Hill was significantly different from Whitehawk and had links with the Kentish Downs and Essex. The explanation may be that the two camps were occupied simultane-ously by different sub-cultures, or that Combe Hill was built and occupied later than Whitehawk.

Musson found little else on Combe Hill. Charcoal, a hearth and some flint flakes showed evidence of occupation, while a few bones showed that oxen and pigs were kept there. There was no sign of a palisade on the short stretch of rampart Musson looked at: in fact no post-holes at all. There is no positive evidence of a massive dipylon on Combe Hill. From the tiny sample of about twenty feet of ditch and bank we would not have expected to find it.

Or are we, even on Combe Hill, looking too far afield? The summit of Windover Hill, immediately above the Giant, was itself a major neolithic site. There is the Windover Long Mound, with its mortuary platform at the north-eastern end overlooking the site of the Long Man. There are three round barrows of uncertain date. The neolithic scarp-crest trackway passes right through the site and is met just to the east of the summit by a terrace-way connecting it with the scarp-foot trackway, also neolithic in date.

Curwen, who described Windover briefly in 1928, identified the terrace-way as a Roman work. He praised the clever engineering which brings it up the escarpment at just the right angle to utilize the upcast of a neolithic flint mine. This kind of thinking is of doubtful value. To begin with, the Romans are traditionally credited with engineering skills not possessed by the natives of these islands. Stonehenge is ample proof of the technical and mathematical skills of the neolithic culture.

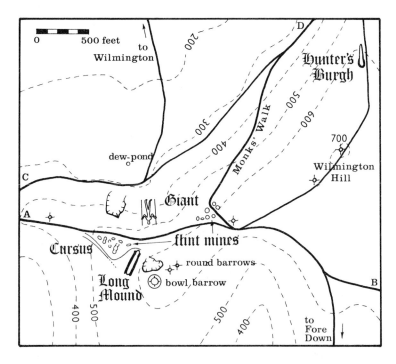

Figure 20.   Map of Windover Hill. The solid black lines are tracks. A-B is the main neolithic ridge-route, the South Downs Way: C-D is the scarp-foot track. Monks' Walk is a diagonal terraceway connecting the two.

At one time, Stonehenge was hailed as a Roman monument for exactly the same reason. The architect, Inigo Jones, wrote notes on the design and origin of Stonehenge which were published posthumously (1655). Jones observed sarcastically that druids had neither academies of architecture nor mathematics lectures and could therefore not have accomplished the design of a building. The early Britons were 'savage and barbarous, knowing no use of garments' and thus incapable of building Stonehenge. At least Jones intuited that the monument was a temple to the sky-god; he thought it was the Roman sky-god Coelus.

There is no reason to suppose that the terrace-way on Windover

Hill was designed or built from the bottom upwards. If the work was done the other way round, the apparent felicity of the route is no longer seen as anything remarkable. The track picks its way down through the flint miners' pits and spoil heaps and then — a very easy piece of engineering — veers eastwards to make a low-angle ramp along the escarpment, meeting the scarp-foot track where it will.

The flint mines, too, prove that neolithic activity concentrated on Windover Hill. There is a cluster of mines near the crest of the escarpment on each side of the Long Man. Although there are several sites along the South Downs where flints were mined in the neolithic, they are all situated on the flint-rich *Actinocamax quadratus* zone of the chalk, which outcrops about one-third of the way down the chalk dip slope: in other words, not on the highest hills looking out over the Weald. Windover seems to be the only site where flint mines were opened in the *Micraster* zone of the chalk. It is also, as far as I am aware, the only site where neolithic miners worked the principal escarpment of the South Downs. This may have been due to the shortage of flints from the conventional *Actinocamax* zone, or some other economic pressure. Alternatively, it may have been felt that arrow-heads taken from a sacred hill top associated with a major deity would be extra potent.

THE WINDOVER CURSUS
One other peculiarity of Windover is a strange linear feature running up the north-western approach to the summit. This well-defined feature, 400 feet long and 30 feet wide, is cambered and flanked by two ditches. Curwen again ascribes the feature to the Roman period; this time it is a Roman road, but again without evidence. The truth is that there is no reason why the Romans should have forced a road up to the summit, if they merely wanted to reach Eastbourne, which is Curwen's explanation. Ivan Margary's more recent and scholarly study of Roman roads shows a perfectly serviceable lowland route from Lewes and Glynde along to a Cuckmere river crossing at Chilver Bridge and then on to Polegate and Pevensey, a major trunk road from which a short spur to Eastbourne would have sufficed.

The short cambered way on Windover Hill that seems to lead nowhere is related instead to the neolithic burial rites that accompanied the building of the Windover Long Mound. This interpretation is linked to the solution of the parallel mystery of the cursus in the Wessex heartland.

The largest and best-known, the Dorset Cursus, is five miles long and probably the most extensive prehistoric monument in Britain. The relatively little known cursus at Stonehenge is two miles long. There are several smaller ones as well; the smallest so far recorded is only 600 feet long, at Northampton. It is common for these mysterious ways with their banks and ditches on each side to begin nowhere in particular and — apparently — end nowhere in particular as well. They have no evident function or geographical relationship with other neolithic relics, except for one. The Dorset Cursus has several long barrows contiguous with it and at right angles to its long axis. At Stonehenge, the cursus is terminated by a long barrow similarly oriented. The cursus is thus associated with the funerary rites of the long barrows and probably functioned as a ceremonial way along which the dead were carried to the mortuary enclosure. It may have been used during the rites for the final interment and the completion of the barrow. Possibly later validatory rituals would have followed the same route to the cenotaph.

Plate 3. The Windover Cursus. This curious double track leads from the South Downs Way at Wind Door to the Windover Long Mound.

The Cursus on Windover Hill is small, but it appears to be a miniature version of the greater ways of the heartland. I measured the Windover Cursus, to see whether the cambered centre was constant in width and also whether the shallow, flat-floored 'ditches' beside it maintained a constant width; this, I hoped, would give an indication of the way in which the cursus was used. The cambered centre was 18 feet wide at the lower, north-western end, narrowing to 14 feet halfway up and 8 feet at the top. This tapering proves that the cambered centre was not a Roman road, which would necessarily have been of constant width. The sunken tracks on each side, recessed up to two feet into the chalk hill side, are 7 feet wide at the lower end and the same at the upper end. The measurements in effect confirm that the Windover Cursus was designed as two sub-parallel tracks with a raised convex reservation separating them. What could these specially-made tracks have been used for?

Like the Stonehenge Cursus, the Windover Cursus leads towards a long barrow. The long axis of the cursus makes an angle of 75° with the main axis of the long barrow. The correspondence is close and the departure from a right angle is easily understood. The approach up the north-western spur is the main control over the orientation of the cursus; the Long Mound, as we saw earlier, relates to the Long Man and its long axis is oriented towards the Long Man's head.

The corpses that were ultimately to be entombed in the Long Mound were carried up the north-west spur of Windover Hill to the site of the south-western end of the Long Mound. When the dead were first brought here, the mound itself had not been built. Instead the bodies were secreted in the mortuary enclosure at the north-eastern end. The northern track veers off to the north just below the Long Mound and then curves back to arrive at the mortuary platform. The southern track leads unambiguously to the south-western end of the Long Mound and may have been used by the celebrants.

The rites associated with the ritual burials were exceedingly elaborate. In Malta, substantial remains of contemporary neolithic temples have survived almost intact: in some cases only the roof is missing. The stone temples at Tarxien, discovered by a farmer in 1913, show by their intricate architecture how complex the rituals were. No stone monuments survive on or near Windover Hill but we can be sure that rituals of similar complexity took place there.

The sunken tracks are consistent with usage by a cart or some other vehicle with a 'wheel' base 4 feet 6 inches wide. The general feeling among archaeologists is that the wheel was not known in the neolithic culture, so the tracks are something of a puzzle. A clue to their origin lies on the distant Mediterranean islands of Malta and Gozo. The bare rock surface near the neolithic temple of Ggantija on Gozo is deeply scored by parallel ruts. The rock-cut grooves are thought to have been made by sleds or slide-cars used for carrying stone blocks to the temple building site.

A sled with its runners in contact with the ground along their entire length would turn relatively slowly, but the grooves on Gozo turn quite sharply. This is consistent with the slide-car, which has runners touching the ground only at the rear ends: the front ends are harnessed to the shoulders of a horse or an ox. It appears that the slide-car may have been in use both on Gozo and on Windover Hill five thousand years ago. A check on the measurements is necessary to confirm the parallel: the distance between the grooves. On Gozo it is 4 feet 6 inches, the same as the Windover tracks. I also measured some grooves leading towards a ruined chambered tomb at Naxxar Gap on Malta. They fluctuated slightly, but always between 4 feet 3 inches and 4 feet 7 inches. Typically, the Naxxar grooves are cut 6 inches into the limestone, about the same as the Windover Cursus. All these pointers tend towards the interpretation of the Windover Cursus as a dual slide-car route to the Windover Long Mound.

All the long barrows were special places: each one was accorded the sanctity of a church. But the unique properties of the Windover Long Mound set it apart from all the other barrows and make it a uniquely sacred site. It is a pity that no modern archaeological dig has been mounted on the complex of features on Windover Hill. A thorough excavation might reveal the post-holes of shrines or even the deep and massive post-holes of a great dipylon. If there were two ritual masts, where would they have stood? Obviously this is pure speculation, but the layout of the site does suggest a natural focus for ceremonies relating to the Long Mound, the Long Man and the summit of the hill.

There is a blank area immediately to the north of the hilltop with its bowl barrow and to the east of the Long Mound. Further north still, the ground falls away steeply to the Giant's Causeway, the western terrace-way. The site suggested for a possible Windover dipylon, on the northern brow of the hill, would make it more conspicuous to the people who were living down in the Weald than a site further back on the summit itself. The putative dipylon site has been wrecked by modern chalk quarrying, so it will never be known what stood or might have stood on that part of Windover Hill. It is a variety of vandalism that is all too common. The ruins of the great Cluniac Priory at Lewes were utterly devastated in the nineteenth century for the sake of a railway cutting.

As far as Windover and the quest for the dipylon gate are concerned, all may not be lost. The case has been made for the Long Man as a neolithic god shown standing at the dipylon gate. It may be that he is shown at the gate of a specific nearby site, and Whitehawk, Combe Hill and Windover Hill are the obvious candidates. There is another possibility, which opens the question out even wider. All the sites considered, whether excavated or not, are on the dry chalk with its long history of utilization for sheep grazing. They are sites which are geomorphologically and pedologically almost frozen in time. The land surface is virtually the same as it was five thousand years ago, up on the chalk downs. It is a very different story down in the valley bottoms and out on the clay lowland. There, soil creep, slope-wash and the occasional river flood have swamped the ancient land surface under several inches and sometimes several feet of silt. On top of that, the dense deciduous forest that once covered the clay vale has smothered it with millennia of autumn leaf falls.

For too long people have made the mistake of equating the present survival of neolithic remains on the chalk hills with the original distribution. There is good reason to suppose that neolithic man made some use of the lowland areas. If we could find more evidence of that lowland activity, some of the mysteries surrounding the barrows, henges and enclosures on the hills might be solved.

All this is leading to the suggestion — it can be put no higher — that the enclosure or shrine with the dipylon gate represented in the Long Man drawing was situated not in the Downs at all but in the lowland to the north.

WILMINGTON, THE WEALD AND THE CARVING OF THE GIANT
If the site was close to Windover Hill, Wilmington churchyard is a natural candidate. Wilmington carries a Saxon name and the village occupies a typical early Saxon site at the foot of the chalk escarpment, enjoying the benefits of easy road communication along the ancient scarp-foot route as well as numerous springs. The water table, or level of water in the chalk, is now fairly low at the upper end of Wilmington village, where the churchyard is situated.

The water in the Priory well is 120 feet below ground level. We must remember that all the evidence from the causewayed enclosures and flint mines points to the neolithic period being significantly wetter. This would have raised the level of saturation in the chalk, so that well levels would have been higher than they are today and the springs would have burst out of the hillside at higher levels.

The slightly elevated position of the churchyard mound, 150 feet above sea level, gives it splendid views. To the south, Windover Hill dominates the view; to the west, north-west, north and north-east, there are extensive and exhilarating views of the Downs and the Weald. This feature of the site would recommend it to neolithic man on aesthetic and spiritual grounds. It would also have been much more convenient than, for example, the summit of Windover Hill as a base for hunting forays into the Vale of Sussex. It is in that area, where landscape development is fairly rapid, that solid archaeological evidence is rare. The Vale is composed mainly of soft clay, which has been worn away in some places to efface the archaeological record; in others, especially the valley floors and other depressions, the old surface has been coated with later deposits. There are no known relics of the neolithic in this area.

In the harder, enduring rocks of Ashdown Forest, some evidence has been preserved. The hard sandstone has been fretted into exotic crags, which make natural shelters. The impressive, tor-like crags at High Rocks near Tunbridge Wells conceal several narrow ravines that sheltered prehistoric man. Firm archaeological evidence from one of the ravines at High Rocks proves that neolithic men were visitors there.

A radiocarbon date of 3700 bc shows that High Rocks was in use as a temporary rock shelter by mesolithic hunters before the neolithic culture developed. Mesolithic man was dependent on hunting, gathering and fishing; he was not a farmer and, having no crops to sow or harvest, nor livestock to tend, was much more mobile than neolithic man. Even so, neolithic remains have been found at High Rocks, resting on top of the mesolithic remains. This indicates that either there was an indigenous Wealden population or people living in the North or South Downs were mobile enough to make hunting trips into the centre of the Weald. Since the clay-bound forests of the Vales of Kent and Sussex would have been extremely wet and sticky underfoot during the neolithic winters, it seems likely that these hunting expeditions took place in the summer or autumn: perhaps in September and October, following the harvest.

Is there anything to link the neolithic hunters visiting the hunting lodge at High Rocks with the neolithic farmers of the East Sussex downs? A few fragments of pottery were discovered with the neolithic occupation layer at High Rocks. They were Ebbsfleet: the same type that was in use at Combe Hill.

High Rocks is not the only place mesolithic and neolithic hunters made use of in this way. There are about thirty other sandstone crags in the centre of the Weald that could have been used as hunting lodges, and some of them have already yielded the tell-tale flint flakes to prove that early man was there, making arrow-heads for the next day's hunting. The rock shelters are concentrated in the Tunbridge Wells area but stretch westwards as far as Balcombe, northwards as far as Chiddingstone and southwards as far as Uckfield, a mere six miles from the South Downs.

This brief glance at the Weald of Sussex is important in restoring some balance in our view of neolithic man's activities. Hunting bands made seasonal expeditions northwards from the downs into the lush, virgin forests teeming with game — roe deer, red deer, wild boar and probably even bison were to be had. Whether they hunted for sport or out of necessity can only be surmised. The very small numbers of wild animal bones found in the causewayed enclosures is suggestive, though. They imply that the game animals were not essential to the neolithic diet. Even if the hunting expeditions were holidays, the presumptive settlement site at Wilmington would have made a very convenient headquarters for these autumn forays.

Wilmington would have had another advantage. Its low site raises the barrows on the summit of Windover Hill to an exalted, reverential level. The Wilmington people may then, while gazing up at the hilltop, have conceived the idea of decorating the hill side itself with a picture of the heroic guardian, the midsummer sun-man who brought light, warmth and a full belly: the guardian who mysteriously activated the magic squares of the arable fields and caused the crops to grow.

THE TRUE CHILDREN OF THE SUN-GOD

So, was it at Wilmington village that the carvers of the Long Man lived? The case seems persuasive, but there is one other possibility, one other site that presents itself as a candidate. It is not as immediately obvious as Wilmington — indeed it may seem surprising. The process of reasoning by which I arrived at this alternative is a very different one from that which led me to Wilmington.

The starting-point was an observation by Drewett (1975) that the typical distance between known neolithic settlements in East Sussex is about 4km (2½ miles) and the inference from this that neolithic clans were farming 'territories' with a radius of 2km (1¼ miles). When mapping the known settlements and then drawing in their hypothetical circular territories, Drewett found that the long barrows tended to occur on or near the boundaries of territories. The reasons for this are not hard to find. If corpses were exposed in the burial grounds before interment in the barrows, these would be places to avoid on grounds of hygiene. As sacred sites, the barrows might have been taboo places, places to be visited only on special occasions. On grounds of hygiene, sanctity or some other taboo, the long barrows were generally constructed away from the occupation sites.

The known occupation sites include the causewayed enclosures at Whitehawk, Offham and Combe Hill, a small rectangular enclosure on the cliff edge at Belle Tout and open 'stances' at Castle Hill in Newhaven, Hobb's Hawth, South Hill on Seaford Head, Bullock Down and Crowlink on the Seven Sisters.

The next stage was to fill in the several blank areas on the map. Nine occupation sites are known to have existed in the Sussex Downs east of Brighton and the blank areas offer space for nine more. Figure 21 shows the most likely fit for the nine lost territories, which we are assuming also had a radius of 1¼ miles. One lost settlement stood in the present built-up area of Peacehaven, another on the flat-topped ridge leading north from Mount Caburn. A third stood on High Hill near Rottingdean: a fourth on Pea Down near Beachy Head. The fifth, sixth, seventh and eighth coincide with later agricultural settlement; one is on Plumpton Plain, one is at Kingston, another is at an undated earthwork on Falmer Hill and another is at Blackcap Farm near Glynde. All the putative occupation sites appear excellently suited for settlement by chalkland farmers.

The ninth of the lost sites is the most significant. Fore Down is a flat-topped hill on the downland dip slope, bristling with a secondary growth of heathy scrub. From Fore Down there is good access along spurs and ridges to the fields and copses of what can now easily be visualized as the Fore Down territory. From the supposed

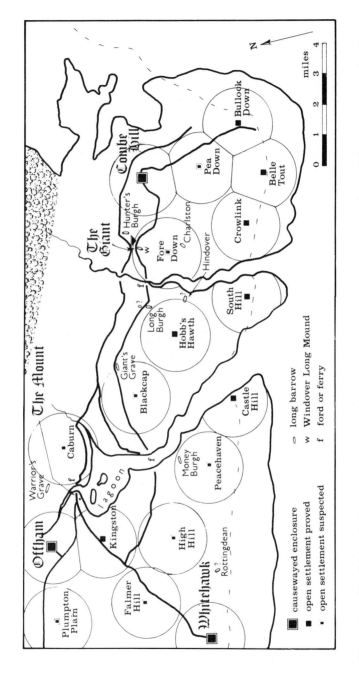

Figure 21. Neolithic tribal territories in the East Sussex Downs. Each territory supported a small farming community. Groups living in the causewayed enclosures acted as hosts for clan gatherings.

settlement site there are splendid views across the entire territory, which extends as far as the Cuckmere, Jevington and Charlston valleys; these low points form natural physiographic boundaries to west, south and east. The view to the northern boundary, the crest of the chalk escarpment, is particularly beautiful. Windover Hill dominates the skyline and is seen rising abruptly from the 300 feet deep, steep-sided dry valley called Deep Dean.

Plate 4.   Fore Down seen across Deep Dean from Windover Hill. A neolithic community living on Fore Down may have carved the Giant on Windover Hill.

The summit of Fore Down is one of the few flat surfaces in the territory and ideal for settlement. Surrounding it, from Oldkiln Bottom across the ridge and over into Deep Dean, is one of the most extensive ancient field systems to be found in Sussex. These fields have been traditionally regarded as Celtic (Jessup, 1970),although hut sites in their midst are known to be Bronze Age. It is probable that some at least of the field boundaries were in use in the Bronze Age, and they may represent a continuity of use from the neolithic. Burgess (1980) points out that so-called 'Celtic' fields that have been found preserved under peat bogs in Ireland were laid out before 3250 BC. Similarly, the ancient field system that can be clearly seen on the hill side south-west of Combe Hill may well date back to the first farmers of Sussex, and thus be contemporary with the causewayed enclosure. It was usual on a Bronze Age farmstead, such as Plumpton Plain, for the ploughed fields to be separated from the settlement by a swathe of open pasture, presumably so that milk cows could be attended to more easily. It seems that this practice, too, may be a neolithic survival, since the same layout occurs at Combe Hill.

Traces of the ancient communication system at Fore Down also survive. Several of the present bridle-ways follow the courses of field-walks and trackways which were established at the same time as the field system. The cross-dyke is overgrown and disused, but it is nevertheless still clearly visible among the gorse bushes.

A cluster of low round barrows on the summit of Fore Down is probably Bronze Age in date. Burgess reminds us that unknown numbers of burial mounds were raised on the sites of abandoned earlier settlements, and it is possible that the Fore Down barrow cluster marks the position of the neolithic occupation site. The association may be a practical one, in that a plot cultivated for too long becomes exhausted and thus usable only for burials. It may, on the other hand, be a religious motive that prompted Bronze Age people to build their graves on cold hearths; the fragile houses of the living give way to the eternal houses of the dead. We should remember that some of the neolithic long barrows, such as Fussell's Lodge in Wiltshire, were built as facsimiles of long houses, with timber walls and doorways.

The effect of the heathy scrub vegetation, which has been preserved on Fore Down, is to reduce wind speeds in the air layer nearest the ground. Far from being an exposed and windswept hill-top in the neolithic, Fore Down, under its original cover of open woodland with cultivated clearings, would have provided a very congenial microclimate which at the same time allowed extensive views in all directions.

The finds on Fore Down so far amount to only a handful of struck flint flakes and an arrow-head, but even these few confirm a neolithic presence. The general trend of the argument, therefore, is that the Fore Down people are likely to have been responsible for the creation of the various monuments on the escarpment where it marks the boundary of the Fore Down territory. It seems in the nature of neolithic projects that they were communal enterprises, so it would seem that the peoples of two or more neighbouring territories would have collaborated to create such a substantial complex of monuments: the two long barrows, the cursus, the (sacred?) flint mines, the diagonal terrace-way and the great drawing of the sun-god. Or it may all have been the work of one small, energetic and spiritually dynamic group.

It is very tempting to see the Fore Down territory, a core of beautifully conserved downland with broad impressive whale-back ridges falling away suddenly in steep scrubland slopes, as a kind of heartland of the neolithic ideal: its shaman devising the ceremonies appropriate to the sacred mount of Windover, its poets and story-tellers evolving sagas of the sun-god, its people closer than any to the central collective mysteries of life, death and the passage of the seasons, fully capable of creating, single-handed, the image of the sun-god. But even if we see the Fore Down folk as the true children of the Giant, there is yet something missing, something unaccounted for. The midsummer sun-god who brings light, warmth and a full belly must be greeted with due ceremony, and that ceremony needs due preparation. The middle of summer must be foreseen with some precision and this, as far as one can tell, was not done at Fore Down, but elsewhere.

10. THE HARVEST HILL

*Summer ends now; now, barbarous in beauty, the stooks rise
Around; up above, what wind-walks! what lovely behaviour
Of silk-sack clouds! has wilder, wilful-wavier
Meal-drift moulded ever and melted across skies?*

Gerard Manley Hopkins, *Hurrahing in Harvest.*

THE CELEBRATION OF SUMMER

If the Long Man is the sun-god arriving to bring High Summer through the ritual gateway to the world of men, how can we know what this meant to the men of the neolithic age? There is ample evidence from the design of Stonehenge, and of the Heel Stone and portal stones in particular, that the summer solstice needed marking as a special occasion. High Summer, which follows the solstice, is the time when the crops ripen and the harvest is begun; it is the crucial time for an agricultural community. The lengthening days, marked out by the sun during the weeks leading up to the solstice, are indicators that the High Summer season is approaching. More than that, it is the sun itself and the warmth it bestows that determine the quality of the harvest.

What could be more natural than a fertility cult based on the annual life cycle of the sun? There is even some evidence that this sun-oriented fertility cult lingered on into the Iron Age. In 350 BC Diodorus Siculus reported that Hecateus of Abdera had written: 'Opposite to the land of the Celts there exists in the ocean an island no smaller than Sicily. The inhabitants honour Apollo more than any other. A sacred enclosure is dedicated to him in the island, as well as a magnificent circular temple adorned with many offerings.' The land of the Celts is Gaul and the island larger than Sicily is apparently Britain. The sacred enclosure dedicated to the sun-god is probably Avebury, since the magnificent circular temple is unmistakably Stonehenge. The passage is unequivocal evidence that the neolithic monuments continued to be religious centres into the Iron Age and moreover that they continued to be places where the sun-god was honoured.

The endurance of some of these elemental nature-responses is remarkable. The celebration of May Day, for example, marking the beginning of summer, goes on now just as it has gone on for at least two thousand years and possibly much longer. May Day is a transformation of the Iron Age feast of Beltane. I vividly remember the May Morning of 1967 in Oxford, when I was Jack-in-Green. Jack-in-Green, or The Tree, is the central fertility symbol of the Morris Dancers' revels, a figure completely covered in fresh foliage and gyrating mysteriously through the city streets at the dawn, not only of that day, but of summer itself. I did not know then that it was Beltane I was celebrating, although I had a strong sense of the sympathetic magic involved. This unconscious continuity of experience can be seen again and again in folk customs. Those who participate in them are unaware or, at best, only partially aware of what they are doing.

Significantly, many of the medieval midsummer revels featured giants as an important part of their ritual. In Salisbury Museum, the twelve-foot-high effigy of a giant with a black bushy beard still survives. At one time the giant was brought out and carried in procession every Midsummer Day, accompanied by a snapping, grotesque figure, the Hobnob. A similar carnival was held at Burford, where a Midsummer Giant was paraded on Midsummer Day, accompanied this time by a dragon.

At Chester, in 1599, the Puritan mayor 'caused the giants in the Midsomer Show to be put downe and broken'. His name — Henry Hardware — marks him out as a born spoiler. Before Mr Hardware's intervention, there had been four giants in the Chester Midsummer Show, as well as a unicorn, a camel, a dromedary, a luce, an ass, a dragon, six hobby horses and six naked boys. Some carnival. The Midsummer celebrations were not just a feature of the backward-looking, rural provinces, either. In London, too, the Midsummer Giants made their appearance every Midsummer Day

Plate 5. The Midsummer Giant of Salisbury, 1887. Though here refurbished in eighteenth-century costume, the head may have been made earlier than 1500. The beadle stands in the centre; the two attendants or 'whifflers' on each side carry the Giant's sword and mace. In front, poised for action, is the Hobnob, the Giant's constant companion.

right through the Middle Ages. An observer in 1589 described them as 'great and uglie Gyants, marching as if they were alive and armed at all points, but within they are stuffed full of brown paper and towe'.

The association of Midsummer pageant-giants with the solstice was very widespread. It is possible that these ferocious painted dummies with their attendant hobnobs and dragons are a distorted memory of the powerful and beneficent sun-god: that the guardian of the neolithic harvest and the gigantic shape of the Long Man himself lived on in this garbled form.

THE HARVEST FEASTS

The arrival of the sun-god in his full glory on 21 June was essential as an inauguration of the crop-ripening season. But is there any evidence that the harvest itself was celebrated by neolithic man? As the focus of the earliest English farmers' secular activities, the harvest must have created feelings of relief, gratitude, self-congratulation and pleasure: feelings that would be likely to find expression in the most joyful feast in the calendar.

The Christian calendar recognizes the Harvest Festival as a major autumn feast. Its ancestry is a very ancient one, with its roots back in the earliest agricultural communities. There is good reason for believing that this was not the only harvest feast; it now seems increasingly likely that the Harvest Festival we are now familiar with was originally the lesser of two feasts. The Christian Harvest Festival is a celebration of the completion of the harvest:

> Come, ye thankful people, come,
> Raise the song of harvest home:
> All is safely gathered in,
> Ere the winter storms begin.

> (Henry Alford)

The words of the harvest hymn are a thanksgiving for the safe gathering of the entire crop. The displays of produce that traditionally decorate churches at this time of the year symbolize the great stores of food safely lardered in the cottager's cupboard and the farmer's barn.

In the early days of farming, however, when the outcome of the harvest was much more uncertain, it was the first produce to be brought in from the fields that prompted the greatest thanksgiving. The First Fruits festival was celebrated on or about 1 August and came to be called Lugnasad by the Celts. The feast probably has its roots in a very early, pre-arable calendar, which survives as the 'Celtic' pastoral calendar. The pastoral calendar has quarter days that are slightly staggered from those of the later arable calendar. The quarter days that evolved later are familiar to us as Lady Day (25 March), Midsummer (24 June), Michaelmas (29 September) and Christmas (25 December).

The original names of the pastoral calendar have been lost, so the later Celtic names will have to be used instead. The pastoral quarter days are Imbolc (1 February), Beltane (1 May), Lugnasad (1 August) and Samhain (1 November). Imbolc, the lambing feast, was incorporated into the Church calendar as Candlemas. Beltane, the time when the summer grazing was considered ready for use, became May Day and it is still a purely pagan celebration. Lugnasad, which may have been the sheep-shearing feast of the pastoral calendar, was assimilated into the Church year as Lammastide. Samhain celebrated the autumn livestock roundup and the slaughter of surplus stock; it was converted into Martinmas. When the First Fruits feast, or Lugnasad, was incorporated into the Christian calendar, biblical support was sought in order to make the pagan associations of Lammastide doctrinally acceptable. Deuteronomy 26 gave the Church exactly what it wanted;

Thou shalt take of the first of all the fruit of the earth which thou shalt bring of thy land that the Lord thy God giveth thee, and shall put it in a basket and shalt go unto the place which the Lord thy God shall choose to place his name there. The priest shall take the basket out of thine hand and set it down before the altar . . . and thou shalt rejoice in every good thing which the Lord thy God hath given thee.

The First Fruits festival has withered under the aegis of the Christian Church, but until the nineteenth century some vestiges still survived. In Scotland, so-called Lammas towers were built in celebration of the First Fruits as late as the eighteenth century. The 'towers' were conical mounds about eight feet high and made of turf. The turf covering is significant; as a fertility symbol the tower had to be an organic, living thing. John Anderson, writing for the Society of Antiquaries of Scotland in 1792, described the building of these towers;

The celebration of the Lammas Festival was most remarkable. Each community agreed to build a tower in some conspicuous place, near the centre of their district, which was to serve as the place of rendezvous on Lammas Day. This tower was usually built of sods . . . tapering to a point at the top which was seldom above seven or eight feet from the ground. In building it, a hole was left in the centre for a flag staff, on which were displayed the colours on the great day of the festival. The tower was usually begun to be built about a month before Lammas, and was carried up slowly by successive additions from time to time being seldom entirely completed till a few days before Lammas, though it was always thought that those who completed theirs soonest and kept it standing the longest time before Lammas, behaved in the most gallant manner, and acquired most honour by their conduct. From the moment the foundations of the tower were laid it became an object of care and attention to the whole community.

Leaving aside the central association between the harvest mounds and Lammastide, there is a curious parallel between the Scottish rites associated with Lammas and an East Sussex custom associated with the next pastoral feast, Samhain. It is well-established that the 'Guy Fawkes' firework celebrations of 5 November are a modern revival of the ancient fire festival traditionally held on 1 November. People in the Lewes area build not Lammas towers but bonfires. As with the Lammas towers these ritual mounds are built in a spirit of friendly rivalry by the 'societies' of each district; each bonfire is a separate, local enterprise, but all are set alight on the same evening of November. While the Lewes Bonfire Societies actively maintain the feast of Samhain, the Lewes site most closely associated with the feast of Lugnasad lies forgotten and neglected.

SILBURY HILL

BBC 2's excavation of Silbury Hill in 1968-69 showed that, buried deep inside the great mound, there is a small conical harvest hill similar to the much later Scottish Lammas towers. At the time of the excavation, which received a great deal of publicity, there was widespread disappointment that the centre of the hill contained nothing more than this. There was no burial chamber, no king accompanied by grave-goods, no artefacts at all. The only clue lay in the structure of the mound itself. There was a radial pattern of ropes laid out under the small core-mound; it was clearly not a burial chamber but a cult object for some other purpose. The organic matter entombed underneath the mound gave a radiocarbon date of 2145 ±95 years bc and even an indication of the season when the mound was raised. The state of the vegetation and the remains of trapped insects showed that the mound was built during the last week of July or the first week of August, thus confirming that Silbury Hill is a gigantic harvest hill (Dames, 1976).

The first Silbury mound was found wanting by its builders. The size of nearby Avebury proves that the area had become a major ritual centre; it is therefore not surprising that Avebury's harvest hill needed to be enlarged to cater for a large community, of whom some at least were probably pilgrims from far away. Silbury was enlarged until it was 130 feet high — a real hill rather than a mere mound. The enormous structure, made mainly of chalk blocks, would have taken some eighteen million man-hours to build. If five hundred men worked on the project during the drier weather of summer and autumn, it would have taken them fifty years to complete. Silbury is, apart from any other significance that it may have, a major monument to the importance of ritual in the neolithic way of life.

In form, Silbury is curious. Obviously, in the 4800 calendar years that have passed since it was built, weathering will have taken its toll. The shape must have been to some extent degraded. Even so, its fundamental elements are still clear and it is thought from the extraordinary internal structure of the mound that its shape has changed very little from the day when it was completed. Silbury was built as a conical hill with the top truncated to make a circular platform on the summit. Near the summit there is a trace of a notch or terrace, which has been interpreted as a remnant of a second ceremonial platform or even part of a path to the summit.

The 1968-69 excavation revealed that the final stage of building, called Silbury III, raised the mound to its present height by a series of stepped stages. Each circular platform was made out of concentric and radial walls of large chalk blocks. As the topmost platform was being completed, Silbury must have looked even more remarkable than it does today: it was a cone made of concentric rostra, each of which was 17 feet high, adding up to a dazzling ziggurat of gleaming, freshly quarried chalk.

It may be that this form, the tiered cone, was selected by the builders because it would give the finished mound absolute stability. The importance of endurance, of everlastingness, to the neolithic spirit is very clear from monuments such as Avebury and Stonehenge. It also seems probable that the shape had some arcane religious significance. The 'built' part of the mound consists of six tiers, and these rest on a seventh, which was cut down into the living rock. The seven-tiered conical mound takes us very close indeed to the design of the Sumerian ziggurat. The Tower of Babel, for example, had seven tiers connected by staircases.

If staircases and terraces were part of the original Silbury design, they were evidently shelved in favour of a smooth surface. The outline was filled in with fine chalk rubble except, rather oddly, for the terrace immediately below the summit platform. On the north-west slope, the outer edge of the terrace below that is just detectable; we can only assume that weathering on the exposed upper slopes of the hill has been responsible for revealing these structural details.

TRACKWAYS LEADING TO SILBURY

What has Silbury Hill to do with the neolithic culture in East Sussex? It may have had a considerable direct impact, since people could have travelled quite easily from Combe Hill, Whitehawk or Wilmington along the neolithic trackways to Avebury. There are chalk trackways dating from the neolithic threading their way along the crest of the South Downs escarpment and also along the foot of the escarpment's steepest slope. The two parallel tracks lead all the way from Beachy Head to the western end of the Downs, where they unite and continue through Hampshire to Winchester. A similar pair of tracks follows the North Downs escarpment. Of these, it is the scarp-foot trackway that has achieved fame as 'the Pilgrims' Way', the route followed by medieval pilgrims on their way eastwards to the shrine of St Thomas at Canterbury. The Pilgrims' Way is nevertheless neolithic in origin. The North Downs trackway joins the South Downs trackway at Winchester and the joint trackway continues to Stonehenge and Avebury. Whether on ponies or on foot, neolithic folk could have completed the one-hundred-mile journey from East Sussex to Silbury Hill in a matter of three or four days.

The direct links between East Sussex and Silbury in the neolithic are not in question; the enduring trackways prove that there was intercourse of some kind between the two areas. Whatever ceremonies took place at Silbury may have taken place there and nowhere else. Certainly the scale of the ceremonies at Silbury was unique. But is it possible that smaller harvest hills were erected elsewhere in neolithic England? If there were other, less striking and less conspicuous harvest hills, is it possible that they have survived unrecognized into the twentieth century?

A HARVEST HILL IN SUSSEX

In order to apprehend our environment, or at least our own limited view of it, we begin with the naming of parts. All that we see must have a name and an explanation: at least a provisional explanation. With the passage of time, the provisional explanation hardens in the mind and is accepted as pure fact. It has always been so. The style of explanation may alter, but once explanations have been applied they tend to adhere. We are thus surrounded by mysteries wrapped in deceptively familiar disguises.

The Priory Mount in Lewes is one such familiar feature. It has been labelled a 'Calvary' and its proximity to the Priory ruins seems to give this medieval Christian interpretation a gloss of respectability. The truth is that the Mount lies *outside* the Priory grounds and is too substantial a monument to be a Calvary. It is a facile explanation of the same type as the 'lazy monk' explanation of the Long Man, and harmless enough except that it has prevented us from seeing the feature with a fresh eye.

So, forgetting for the moment the problems of explanation or interpretation, let us look at the shape of the hill. Approached from Lewes railway station the Mount is inauspiciously hidden behind Mountfield House. It is only from the car park on its eastern side or the recreation ground on its southern side that it can be seen clearly.

The Mount is a steep-sided conical mound forty-two feet high. The apex of the cone is missing so that the summit is a circular platform twenty feet in diameter. The base is nearly exactly circular, with a diameter of 170 feet. The entire mound is turf-covered, but the interior is composed of chalk. The sides are inflected by a spiral path seven feet wide, indicating that the mound was originally approached from the north, i.e. from Mountfield Road. This access is now cut off by the garden of Mountfield House and also by the bowling green, which has encroached into the south-western quadrant of the Mount, making the original path impassable. The removal of part of the Mount to make space for the bowling green is an astonishing piece of vandalism.

How is the Mount to be interpreted? The Calvary idea can be put aside for the reason already mentioned. Hadrian Allcroft has suggested an alternative view that it may be a Norman motte. More specifically, he identifies it as the first defensive motte built by William de Warrenne after the Norman Conquest. There are three reasons for discounting this view. The first is that the Castle itself

Plate 6. The Mount in Lewes. The steps and narrow tarmac path leading to the left are modern; part of the original grassy spiral path can be seen higher up.

comprises two mottes on excellent natural eminences, and there is no reason to look for more on lower and less defensible ground. The second cause for doubt is the form of the Mount, which has no ditch surrounding it, so that it could not have been intended as a defensive structure. Its summit diameter is also too small to have carried a significant defensive work. Even allowing for possible denudation, the platform could never have been more than 25 feet across. This compares very poorly with 80 feet at Bramber Castle and 90 feet at Arundel Castle. Allcroft was aware of this weakness in his argument and declared, rather desperately, that Warrenne was too poor to build a larger motte. The absurdity of this is too patently obvious to press home; it is enough to observe that Warrenne was the wealthiest land-owner in East Sussex, holding as many as forty-three manors.

A third objection to the Norman motte interpretation of the Mount is that it is down far too close to the floodplain level of the River Ouse to have been any use as a defensive position. Allcroft was supported in his military view of the Mount by Lieut-Col. D. Macleod (1939), who pointed to another, analogous, mound, the Twineham Mound, which shows a similar setting with a Priory and water meadows nearby. Macleod noted that the Twineham Mound, like the Priory Mount, is close to a monastic foundation; he nevertheless supported the idea that both mounds were designed to carry castles.

If the comparisons with Silbury Hill hold good, the Priory Mount in Lewes had an altogether different function. The similarities between the two structures are quite impressive:

1. Both are artificial hills.
2. Both are made of chalk.
3. Both are turf-covered.
4. Both are conical with the apex of the cone cut off.
5. Both have a circular platform at the summit.
6. Both have side slopes at c.30° (Silbury 29°, Mount 31°).
7. Both have ledges or ways below the summit.
8. Both have valley-floor sites with wetlands close by.
9. Both have a base diameter/height ratio of 4.0.

There are, of course, important differences. Silbury is much higher: 130 feet compared with the Mount's 42 feet. Its base diameter is much broader: 520 feet compared with the Mount's 170 feet. Silbury's ledge appears to be circular and a relic of the hill's structural design, whereas the Mount has a well-preserved spiral way, most of which is still negotiable. The small size of the Mount incidentally precludes another medieval explanation for the Mount. It has been suggested that the Mount is a spoil heap and that it was created more or less as a by-product of the excavation of the Dripping Pan, a medieval salt pan immediately to the east of the Mount. The volume of the Mount is too small for this to be the case. The present size of the Dripping Pan, which is now a football ground, shows that some 936,000 cubic feet of material were dug from the site. The volume of the Mount, at 558,000 cubic feet, accounts for only half of the excavated material.

In spite of the significant differences between the Mount and Silbury, the similarities are powerfully suggestive. If we suppose that the Mount is a neolithic harvest hill of the same general type as Silbury, can the differences be explained? The difference in size is the most obvious: it is the quality that has drawn so much attention and publicity to Silbury and allowed the Mount to moulder in

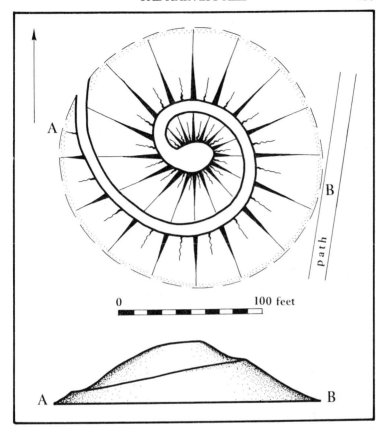

Figure 22.   The Priory Mount in Lewes: plan and profile. The Mount is shown in its original state, although now the spiral path is intercepted by a short modern path approaching from the south.

oblivion. It is also the easiest difference to explain. Silbury was situated close to the nerve centre of the neolithic culture of southern Britain, with Avebury and later Stonehenge near at hand. Since this was the meeting-place of several trackways and ritual gatherings may have attracted large numbers of people, the harvest hill would need to be especially large.

By contrast, the neolithic cell in East Sussex was a smaller nucleus, possibly a community of only a thousand or two. Their ritual centres would be proportionately modest, and a small harvest hill would suffice. It is interesting to note that Silbury Hill is exactly three times higher than the Mount. If the proportions were arrived at deliberately, what on earth could the ratio 1:3 signify? Were there, perhaps, *grades* of harvest hill?

The Mount has never been the subject of an archaeological dig, so no internal evidence of date is available. Even so, the section of modern path cutting into the southern flank of the Mount has exposed a fragment of bone which supports a neolithic date. The shoulder blade of a cow or an ox was buried about a foot below the original surface. It was the custom for workmen to bury their tools near the surface of ritual monuments as the work was completed. A cache of antler picks was found two feet down from the summit of the neolithic Marlborough Mound in 1912. Similar deposits of antler picks and ox-bone shovels were found in the bank and ditch at Avebury (Burl, 1979).

THE SPIRAL PATH

Numbers, shapes and geometry were important concepts in the neolithic mind, although quite what some of the number and shape relationships can have meant is probably lost to us for ever. It is like the tantalizing graffiti found in the flint mines at Harrow Hill, or the 'chessboard' from Whitehawk. What exactly was the writing intended to mean? Sometimes when we see artefacts as inscrutable as these we can feel the cold draught of the alienating centuries that separate us from the carvers and builders of the New Stone Age. They become suddenly as distant and as unknowable as the denizens of another planet. Perhaps it is as well, on occasions, to feel the full force of the fifty centuries that have passed. Their values were different from ours in so many important ways.

It is useful to remember this when assessing the meaning of the spiral path to the summit of the Mount. The spiral seems to distinguish the Mount from Avebury, although it may be that the original ziggurat had a spiral ramp connecting the seven levels before the smooth facing was applied. What was the spiral path for? The obvious answer — to provide a way to the summit — is almost certainly not the complete answer.

This much can be said with confidence, because the spiral is known to have been a very powerful symbol in the neolithic. It is carved again and again on the slabs lining the passage-grave of New Grange and there is an elaborate triple linked spiral in the place of honour. On the wall of the central chamber it awaits its annual illumination. Just once a year, on the winter solstice, the sun shines through a specially constructed slot over the door lintel, along the passage and lights up the triple spiral. Each of the three spirals is itself a double spiral, and the whole design makes a maze, although a rather simplified version of the (probably contemporary) turf mazes which still survive at Saffron Walden in Essex, Hilton in Cambridgeshire, Wing in Rutland and Alkborough in Lincolnshire.

From New Grange we learn that the spiral is associated with the sun and the sun's perilous journey through time and space. On a different level, the spiral design is generally believed to represent the journey inwards, the dissolution of the conscious mind and therefore, by extension, the journey of self-discovery, the dominance of the unconscious spirit and death itself. To the Stone Age mind, it would thus be a symbol of enormous power, a symbol of the path to the other world: and that in its turn might be the after-life or the ecstatic world-within-this-world of the seer or the prophet.

Not all the spirals employed by neolithic man were carved or built. Natural spirals were sometimes pressed into service as well. For example, at Stoney Littleton chambered barrow in Somerset, a fine ammonite cast has been incorporated into one of the door jambs. The spirals carved in stone are small, mostly only a hand's breadth across. But larger spirals exist, as the plan of the Trundle causewayed enclosure shows. The massive, nine-sided earthwork which now dominates the site is a later Iron Age structure, which covers and therefore obscures the outermost bank of a much earlier neolithic enclosure. The later occupation has done much to disguise and disrupt the original plan of the banks, but it has been clear for fifty years, since the Curwen excavation of 1929, that a major part of the bank system was a partial spiral. It seems possible that the *whole* plan may have been based on a spiral design, and it is possible to reconstruct it as such.

Neolithic man chose to draw a large spiral path on the Trundle, whether as part of the enclosure design or as the complete design. The elemental ingredients of the Trundle site are not so dissimilar to those of the Mount. Both sites are marked by a spiral path. Whereas the Mount is an entirely artificial hill for the spiral path to climb, the Trundle's spiral enclosure was located right on the summit of a natural hill, St Roche's Hill, which reaches 677 feet. In both cases, the path spirals inwards and upwards and the centre is the highest point. The metaphor is as obvious today as it must have been then. The spiral mount symbolizes the journey towards self-

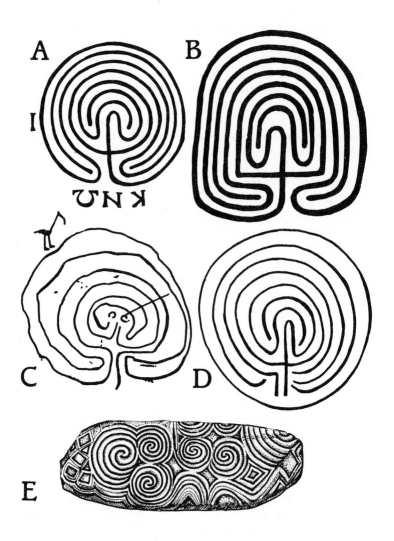

Figure 23. The neolithic maze. A: tetradrachm coin from Knossos, where the Labyrinth was the home of the Minotaur, *c*.1500 BC. B: 'Mother Earth' symbol of the Hopi Indians, modern. C: rock engraving, Val Camonica, Italy, *c*.2500 BC. D: rock engraving, Tintagel, Cornwall, *c*.2000 BC? E: kerbstone at New Grange; the vertical slot marks the path followed by the rays of the midwinter sunrise as they penetrated to the central chamber, 3300 BC.

fulfilment, ecstasy and death, by spiralling inwards, and the union of earth, sky and man by spiralling upwards. The symbolic significance of the return journey is equally clear; after gaining self-knowledge, man returns to the everyday world of action; after death, there is rebirth. It is a re-working of the complex of ideas associated with the long barrows.

With these weighty symbols adhering to it, the spiral was bound to appear somewhere in East Sussex, on some scale, whether small or large. It is not surprising that the spiral should have been incorporated into the design of the sacred Mount.

THE MOUNT AND THE BROOKLAND LAGOON

The Lewes harvest hill with its spiral path certainly seems incongruous now, standing on a confined site hemmed in by a bowling green, a tennis court, a car park, two houses and a railway cutting. There is nothing here of the grandiose and spacious atmosphere surrounding Silbury, Stonehenge or the Ring of Brodgar. In order to see the Mount as it was originally intended, we must imagine all the ephemera of present-day Lewes stripped away, leaving only the downland turf curving gradually up from the mound to the summit of Mount Harry, itself as yet unstained with the English blood that drenched it during the great battle between de Montfort and Henry III in 1264.

From Mount Harry, traffic on foot and horseback along the South Downs Way wore a white path towards the River Ouse. Somewhere near here the prehistoric track found a place where the river could be crossed. What manner of crossing it was can only be guessed. A ford seems possible only if the river was broader and shallower then; a bridge only seems less likely because no remains of neolithic bridges have been found in this region, but we should remember the impressive Tarr Steps on Exmoor, which are thought to date from this era. A third possibility is a corduroy road, which is a causeway made of logs laid side by side across a floodplain to ensure a firm and dry footfall.

One problem in reconstructing the ancient landscape is that the hydrology of the Ouse floodplain, like that of the other Sussex rivers, has changed very significantly since the neolithic. To begin with, the layer of clay and silt that makes up the top forty feet of the floodplain has been deposited within the last six thousand years. Some of it is peaty, and has therefore developed *in situ*; but much of it is soil washed down from the Wealden clearings created by many generations of farmers; it is the indirect product of soil erosion. The solid floor of the valley between Lewes and the sea would thus have been lower than it is today. We also have to visualize the level of the sea altering in relation to that solid floor. The sea had almost reached its present level about five thousand years ago, after rising in fits and starts from about three hundred feet down. When we put these two processes together, we can see that the Ouse valley would have been an arm of the sea about five thousand years ago, with a water surface about twenty-five feet below the present land surface of the floodplain at Lewes.

The Brooks south of Lewes were therefore a broad, circular lagoon, ebbing and flowing with the tides but perfectly sheltered by the encircling hills. The 'bottle-neck' to the north of the Brooks, where the Ouse emptied into the lagoon, would have been the southernmost point at which the valley could have been crossed on foot, perhaps by corduroy road at low tide. It is also possible that a ferry operated here. Concentrations of dugout canoes and plank boats at North Ferriby are strongly suggestive of a major ferry service across the Humber Estuary in 2000 BC (Burgess, 1980). The narrower estuary of the Ouse would have been no great obstacle. Even so, the narrowest point would have been chosen, in the vicinity of the Mount. It looks very much as though Southover High Street and its continuation in Mountfield Road represent the original neolithic route to the river crossing.

Michael Dames, in his book on Silbury Hill, reminds us that the broad and silted ditch round the hill was once a shallow lake. The mound is the womb of the Earth Mother which produces the harvest. The water surrounding the mound may represent the waters of the womb itself; as such it has to be seen as an integral part of the landscape symbolism of the fertility cult. Dames thinks that the mound should be seen reflected in the still waters of its moat.

The Mount site, only 250 feet from the northern shore of a sheltered, calm, lagoon-like estuary, takes on an additional ritual significance in the light of Dames' remarks. In purely aesthetic terms alone, the Mount in its original setting must have been a magnificent and moving sight, whether seen from the trackways on the surrounding hills or from dugout canoes on the lagoon. From the low level of the lagoon, the Mount would rise from its low, narrow peninsula as if floating on the still water. Like certain other neolithic sites, this is a place with peculiarly intimate associations with water. The Ring of Brodgar is located on a narrow isthmus between two peaceful lochs. Waulud's Bank at Luton is a D-shaped earthwork which marks the source of the River Lea. Silbury Hill is very close to the principal source of the River Kennet.

In order to see how closely the Mount was integrated into the neolithic landscape, a check for intervisibility was run. As we saw earlier, the sight-lines that connect the long barrows appear to have been assessed very carefully when their locations were being selected. The Mount can be seen from three long barrows. The sight-lines to the Warrior's Grave and the Giant's Grave are easy to prove. The sight-line to Money Burgh appears initially to be interrupted by Upper Rise, a curious oval hill which rises abruptly out of the floodplain immediately to the south of the Mount and attains a height of 64 feet above sea level. In fact, the sight-line between Money Burgh and the Mount just clears the summit of Upper Rise. It is one of the many 'coincidences' of neolithic geometry that the summit of Upper Rise lies precisely on the sight-line.

A little further to the south-east is Lower Rise, which is even more remarkable because the main part of it is almost circular in plan and perfectly convexo-concave in profile. Lower Rise is smaller in area, but reaches a height of 84 feet. There is no known geo-morphological explanation for these apparently natural islands of chalk immersed in the silts of the River Ouse. What is certain, though, is that they would both have been true islands in the neolithic period, at least at high water.

Apart from adding greatly to the beauty of the lagoon, Upper and Lower Rise may have held some religious significance in the neolithic fertility cult. Clearly they were not used as harvest hills; in spite of their impressive size, there would have been no point in having two or three such hills in close proximity, and it is evident from the very elaborate internal structure of Silbury that the harvest hills had to be *built*. What function, if any, the islands had in neolithic times will probably never be known. Perhaps excavation of their summits would reveal traces of henge-like structures or some other edifice, such as a ritual pylon; but there is no surface evidence of anything at all having been built on either island.

Returning to the safety of the mainland, we can be surer of the Mount's links with other neolithic sites. The radiating sight-lines were spiritual and conceptual links, but not lines along which people would necessarily travel. In order to prove neolithic activity at the Mount, we need to establish that the Mount lay on at least one neolithic route.

JUGGS' ROAD

The Mount is situated on a tongue of slightly raised ground projecting from the western valley side towards the River Ouse. The axis of Southover High Street and its continuation along Mountfield Road occupies the crest of this low ridge. The route seems to aim for the lowest putative crossing point on the River Ouse in the neolithic period. Mountfield Road passes within a few yards of the Mount and, if the hunch is right, it conceals a neolithic trackway. All we have to do is to follow it.

The modern course of Southover High Street continues more or less straight to the west through Southover; then it makes an abrupt southward turn to become the A275 to Newhaven. Right on the corner, an obscure side road continues the original line of Southover High Street: this peaceful little by-way is called Juggs' Road. Its odd name relates to a phase in its history when it was used by Brighton fishermen, or juggs, to bring their catches to Lewes.

Juggs' Road has been diverted for a short distance between Lewes and Kingston, where the deep cutting for the new A27 has been made. Juggs' Road crosses this by means of an elegant and new, if rather incongruous, concrete bridge. The rest of the route has the savour of a very ancient way. It wanders slightly, first to left and then to right, just as we might expect of a track laid out by a largely pedestrian culture, yet it rarely wanders more than two hundred yards on either side of its mean direction, which shows a highly developed consciousness of the geography of the area. The track has a strangely purposeful feeling. The first stretch, although a quiet and narrow by-way, has been carefully made up with tarmac. This quickly gives way to a raw, stony track, sometimes hedged on one side, sometimes completely buried in foliage to make a tunnel-like green lane, and sometimes wide open to distant downland views, as it was for countless centuries.

So the road goes on, through Kingston Hollow, up the steep escarpment by means of the diagonal bostal typical of these ancient ways, over Castle Hill and on to Bevendean. Once the road has struggled up Castle Hill, it remains up on the hill tops and high cols, always above five hundred feet. After passing through the outskirts of Woodingdean, where the track is made up again, Juggs' Road is transformed into Brighton Race Course. At the halfway point along

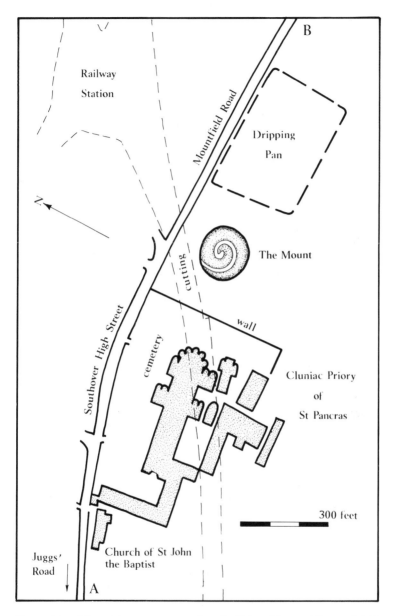

Figure 24. Map of the area surrounding the Priory Mount. The road A-B follows part of the neolithic route from Whitehawk to the Ouse river crossing.

Plate 7. Juggs' Road. Part of the neolithic ridgeway leading from Whitehawk to the Mount, close to the neolithic occupation site of Falmer Hill.

the race course, the ancient way splits into three; or rather it is impossible to see immediately which of the three modern routes conceals the ancient road.

But there, less than a mile away to the south-west, is the key to this small mystery and, what is more, the confirmation that the ancient way is indeed neolithic in age. The southernmost of the three ways, which is incidentally the only one of the three to remain at hill top level on this exposed and windswept ridge, is the race course itself, which leads, just to the south of the grandstand, right into the neolithic causewayed enclosure of Whitehawk.

For most of its six-mile distance Juggs' Road is a ridge route, and that in itself gives it a kinship with other neolithic trackways. Although not by any means straight, it avoids unnecessary detours and completes a crow-flight journey of 6.125 miles, the distance between the Mount and Whitehawk, in 6.25 miles; the road is thus only 2 per cent longer than the straight-line route — a degree of straightness achieved by few twentieth-century roads. The purpose of Juggs' Road was to join the Whitehawk causewayed enclosure to the main neolithic route in Sussex, the South Downs Way. At the node or confluence of the two important tracks were two major features, the one natural and the other man-made: the lowest crossing place on the River Ouse and the Harvest Hill.

11. THE TIMEPIECE OF
THE GREEN KING

When you rise in the eastern horizon
You fill every land with your beauty.
Though you are far away, your rays are upon earth;
Though you are in the faces of men, your footsteps are unseen.
The world and its creatures subsist in your hand,
Even as you have made them.
When you have risen they live,
When you set they die;
For you are length of life,
And men live through you.

Ikhnaton, 'Hymn to Aton'.

THE MOUNT AS AN OBSERVATORY

There were no structures on the scale of the great monuments of
Avebury or Stonehenge in East Sussex. Nevertheless, we must
remember that at Stonehenge celestial observations were made in
conjunction with the surrounding landscape and sky; it was the
interrelation of viewpoint, marker-posts or -stones, horizon, sun
and moon that made up the complete instrument. At Stonehenge,
the viewpoint and markers were concentrated in the centre, while
the horizon and the sky were necessarily far beyond. At the Mount,
a significantly different arrangement has meant that the true
function of the monument has never been fully realized. The
Mount itself was the centre of an observatory, but it was only a
viewpoint: no orientations are apparent. The markers for the

Mount were instead located far out on the horizon, against the sky itself.

The important solar and lunar observations made at Stonehenge may have served the neolithic peoples of Southern England generally, but it is more likely that the principal observations — especially those that fixed the key points in the solar calendar — were made locally at many sites. The Mount at Lewes would have made an ideal, local, solar observatory, with site qualities that are unique in Sussex. The Brookland basin provided the clear space across which the observations could be made without any obstruction; the encircling walls of the chalk escarpment enclose the Mount with flat-summited hill crests. Together, these features of the site ensured that a clean and smooth local horizon was always available for accurate observations. The artificially raised summit of the Mount offered a clear view above the tops of any trees that might have fringed the still lagoon.

The Mount is, in addition, marked by its spiral path as a probable sun monument. There are ancient legends that the sun-king, on his death, went to a spiral castle; the image links the idea of sunset with death and the beginning of a maze-like journey through the unknown darkness. In a rite based on the same death and rebirth allegory, initiates to the Eleusinian Mysteries had to pass through a maze in order to be reborn. It is thought by some that Glastonbury Tor was laid out as a spiral maze to show that it was the entrance to the underworld. Gwyn, king of the fairies, was supposed to dwell on the Tor. Gwyn was also the lord of Annwn, the place where departed souls gathered in readiness to go off to the underworld. The Mount, with its spiral path, will have acquired some of these associations, but before they were transformed into the late, effete form of the Celtic fairy stories that are familiar to us today.

The hypothesis that the Mount functioned not only as a harvest hill but also as a solar observatory is not an easy one to verify. On the other hand, there is one date in the calendar that is known to have been of paramount importance in the farming year from neolithic times onwards; the day is, of course, the summer solstice. If the Mount was intended by its builders to be a sun monument, the sunrise position on the summer solstice should be marked in some way.

At Stonehenge, the Avenue, Heel Stones and the fallen portal stones were designed to mark out the precise alignment from the centre of the circle to that point on the horizon where the sun rises on 21 June; or, to be more accurate, where the sun rose on the summer solstice during the neolithic period. Professor Gerald Hawkins has calculated that the summer solstice sunrise alignment (assumed to pass through the Heel Stone) was correct in 1500 B.C. The sunrise positions change gradually over long periods owing to small alterations in the relationship between the tilt of the earth's axis and the plane of its orbit. For the last nine thousand years, the sunrise and sunset positions have been moving along the horizon to the south at a rate of about one-fiftieth of a degree per century, or approximately one degree every five thousand years. With this correction in mind, it is possible to make a modern observation of a solstice sunrise and then convert it, by calculation, into a neolithic quasi-observation.

THE SOLSTICE GLORY

From the Mount on 21 June 1980, the sun was seen to rise over Cliffe Hill at a point 59° East of Magnetic North. Five thousand years ago, we know that the sunrise position was one degree further north. The neolithic position is marked by a round barrow, but it is questionable whether that should, on its own, be taken as significant, since there are several round barrows scattered along the horizon. *One* coincidence of this kind can be explained away as pure chance.

There was, however, an entirely unexpected and dramatic pre-sunrise event that may hold a greater significance. As the sun rose over the true horizon beyond Cliffe Hill, at a lower level and to the north of the local sunrise, vertical rays of light shot through the clear dawn air and back-lit the skyline just to the south of the Warrior's Grave long barrow. It was an awe-inspiring sight and infinitely more magical than the local sunrise that followed some twenty minutes later. Again, knowing that there has been a south-ward shift in the true sunrise position since the neolithic creation of the cenotaph, we can see that the 'glory' that now lights up the hill crest just south of the Warrior's Grave would have lit up the earthen long barrow itself five thousand years ago.

The implications are obvious. The true sunrise glory marks out a clear neolithic alignment connecting the long barrow, the solstice sunrise and the Mount. It lends strong support to the interpretation of the Mount as a neolithic monument and shows that the siting of at least one of the two landmarks — either the long barrow or the Mount — involved a consideration of the alignment with the

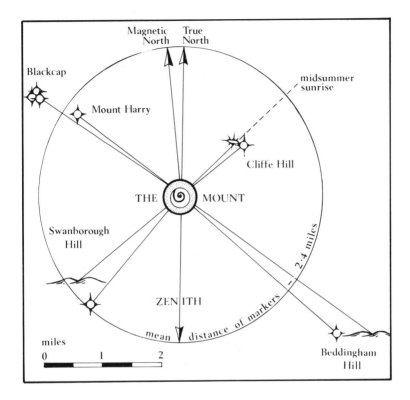

Figure 25. The Brookland solar observatory. The orientations to midwinter and midsummer sunrises and sunsets have been calculated for 3000 BC.

solstitial sunrise. Since the Mount is the viewpoint of the observatory, it is more likely to be the earlier structure of the two, although the building of the marker may have followed within a matter of months.

Why should the alignment have been established at all? Certainly the design of the observatory's structures was very modest when compared with the design of Stonehenge. One possibility is that the more complex and advanced calculations concerning the cycles of the moon were left to the astronomer-priests of Stonehenge. Alternatively — and this seems more probable — the Mount observatory was developed before Stonehenge and was therefore based on simpler astronomical concepts.

Markers to show the sunrise and sunset positions of the summer and winter solstices would have been comparatively straight-forward to set out. Careful observations for a few weeks at midsummer and midwinter were all that was necessary. After the two short periods of trial and error, when temporary posts were set up to mark successive solar events along short stretches of skyline, the positions were established for all time, or at least for the duration of the neolithic civilization. The markers are still only one degree out at most; it has proved a very accurate timepiece.

THE GREEN CLOCK-FACE

We have now to establish why Lewes should have been chosen as the location for a solar observatory. Given that other monuments show a preference for exposed and elevated sites with spectacular views, we might have expected a hilltop site for this important mound. Indeed, the mound would for all practical purposes have been redundant if the whole enterprise had been conducted from the summit of Mount Caburn.

We must not lose sight of the hill's other function as a harvest hill; the built mound was necessary for the August rite. The valley floor site in the Brookland basin, down beside the waters of the lagoon, can also be explained in terms of the association of ideas discussed in the last chapter. The mound needed to be close to water; even under the wetter conditions that are known to have prevailed in the neolithic, that requirement would automatically exclude the upper slopes of the chalk hills.

Yet there is more to recommend the physical geography of the downland that surrounds the Mount. The principal, and unique, property of this particular site is that the local horizon is just two or three miles from the Mount in each of the directions where solstitial events were observed. The crests of the valley sides surrounding the Brooks bring the local horizon close enough to have provided the astronomer-priests with clear-cut and smooth skylines on which they could sight; distant and misty prospects, however appealing aesthetically, could not be relied on to give precise observations.

The conditions described here could be found, in very general terms, in the other downland water gaps. What is exceptional about the Ouse valley is the constriction of the valley to north and south of the two-mile-wide wetland basin called the Brooks. This circular basin is almost entirely confined by impressive escarpments, each of which provides a smooth and unmistakable crest line for observation.

The Caburn massif to the east supplies a surveying table for the midsummer sunrise. Mount Harry to the west could be used to mark the midsummer sunset. Beddingham Hill to the south-east and Castle Hill to the south-west could be used to mark the midwinter sunrise and sunset respectively. If these were the considerations — and it certainly seems as if they were — the Mount site at Lewes was an ideal choice. No other site in Sussex could have suited the requirements so well.

Observations of present-day sunrises and sunsets can easily be made into simulations of neolithic events. All that needs to be done is to subtract one degree from the present compass reading, and the position of the neolithic rising or setting in 3000 BC can be ascertained. The tables below show the alignments and declinations of four major neolithic solar events.

SOLAR EVENTS ON THE TRUE HORIZON

Sunrise/Sunset	Bearing	Alignment	Distance (miles)
Midsummer SR	54.5°	Cliffe Hill Warrior's Grave	1.25
Midsummer SS	312.5°	Mount Harry round barrow	2.50
Midwinter SR	131.5°	Firle-Beddingham col	4.00
Midwinter SS	237.5°	Swanborough-Castle Hill col	2.25

SOLAR EVENTS ON THE LOCAL HORIZON

Sunrise/Sunset	Bearing	Alignment	Distance (miles)
Midsummer SR	58°	Cliffe Hill round barrow	0.75
Midsummer SS	309°	Blackcap barrow cluster	3.00
Midwinter SR	136.5°	Beddingham Hill summit barrow-site	3.50
Midwinter SS	227°	Swanborough Hill summit barrow-site	2.50

Mean 2.4 miles

The short distances involved in these alignments were essential. Observations had to be made in conditions of variable and unpredictable visibility, and without the aid of binoculars or telescopes. The mean distance of 2½ miles between the markers and the Mount guaranteed good, accurate observations with the naked eye.

The coincidence of both sets of alignments with important landscape features such as cols and summits, or with neolithic and Bronze Age barrows is very close indeed. In some places the natural horizon supplied the markers that were needed; in others, barrows were used. It was an elegant and economical solution to a challenging surveying problem: but then, it is no more than we should expect of this gifted and ingenious people.

If such a highly sensitive response to the landscape seems alien to us, we should remember that there are peoples who, even in the twentieth century, react in much the same way. It was only after I had discovered how the Brookland skyline could function as an accurate calendar that I learnt of the Hopi Indians' very similar use of their skyline. The traditional Hopi way of life is, significantly, intensely ceremonial and the well-being of crops, livestock and people is seen as utterly dependent on an elaborate cycle of calendrical rites. The complicated rites involve the masked impersonation of animals and ancestors as well as singing and dancing.

It is essential that the Hopi identify exactly the right date for the ritual appropriate to each event in the farming calendar, from the planting of early corn to the main harvest. The correct dates are indicated by the position of the rising sun on the eastern horizon. All the key dates in the farming year are associated with some distinctive natural landform; the landforms in turn have acquired the names of the rituals, which are also the Hopi words for the calendar dates. It is the job of a shaman, the Sun Watcher, to observe the sunrise positions, warn his neighbours of the approach of important dates and, in due course, announce them. When the sun rises in a distinctive valley notching the skyline, the Sun Watcher announces that it is 'lohalin', 21 June, and time for the summer solstice ceremony. The last corn planting must follow within four days (Forde, 1934).

The Hopi also employ a sacred symbol, which is the mirror image of the rock-carved spiral image, thought to be Bronze Age, at Tintagel. This curious parallelism of thinking, like the use of the skyline as a solar calendar, points the way towards an evolutionist view rather than a diffusionist view of prehistory. Only the most eccentric prehistorian would wish to develop the notion that there had been contact between neolithic or Bronze Age Europeans and the Hopi Indians. It is much more likely to be a case of like conditions producing like results.

The Mount in Lewes has lain forgotten and neglected for too long. In spite of its great antiquity and in spite of the degradation of its skyline markers, it can still function today, just as it did five thousand years ago, like the stoutly-made mechanism of an antique clock. It requires neither electricity nor clockwork to make its slow, invisible hands sweep inexorably round the horizon. Farm carts and floods, hurricanes and haymakers alike may pass across the five-mile diameter of the dial without disturbing its working, driven as it is by silent earth- and sun-power. This truly was, and still is, the green clock-face of the Green King: the timepiece by which the guardian-god was held to his covenant that he would return at the summer solstice. But it was even more than this; it was the circular sacred bower into which the god was welcomed and from which his benevolent, fertilizing power could emanate, to bring ripe grain and dry hay in plenty.

12. THE GUARDIAN-GOD

Kouros most great, Dikte for the year, O march and rejoice in the dance and song that we make to you with harps and pipes mingled together, and sing as we come to a stand at your well-fenced altar ... Kouros the great, to us leap for full jars, and leap for fields of fruit, and leap for fleecy flocks, and for hives to bring increase.

Stone stele in eastern Crete, about AD 150.

THE RESTORATION OF A MYTH

Neolithic man chose the sites for his sacred monuments with care and sensitivity on a scale that is all but incomprehensible to us. Only by reconstructing the ancient geography of Sussex and seeing the archaeological sites within the context of the ancient landscape have we begun to appreciate his deep understanding of the inter-action of hills, sky and water. When we look closely at the site of each monument, the natural logic of the choice becomes apparent, both in the context of landscape aesthetics and in the context of neolithic religious values. Thus it is that important new elements in neolithic culture have surfaced, and it is now possible to assemble the rudiments of neolithic myth. In certain ways, inevitably, that myth will be seen as foreshadowing mythic elements that we know from the Bronze Age and later; in other ways, it will be different from anything else that we know.

Mephistopheles gave Faust a key. We too have been given a key to unlock the mystery: the Giant's staves, which represent the great gate-posts perhaps of Whitehawk, Combe Hill or some nearby lowland enclosure. None of the posts remains standing. Even at Stonehenge, where the ritual gate-posts were blocks of stone instead of xylons, only one remains and that is fallen: Stone 95, the misnamed Slaughter Stone. At least at Stonehenge there is clear proof that the portal stones were designed, along with the Heel Stones and the Avenue, to honour the arrival of the sun-god at the summer solstice, and to inaugurate the season of High Summer.

Although we cannot be sure what kind of ceremony marked the solstice, it must have been a time of rejoicing, thanksgiving and possibly sacrifice. The modern, so-called druidical ceremonies that take place annually at Stonehenge are not likely to be authentic. The nearest we can get are the Hymns to Aton, written by the Pharaoh Ikhnaton in the second millennium BC. This Bronze Age king is often seen as a modernizing influence, attempting to replace polytheism with monotheistic sun-worship. He may, alternatively, be regarded as backward-looking, in the sense that his sun-god seems to come close to the solitary male deity worshipped in the neolithic, although it must be emphasized that a goddess also figured large in the neolithic scheme. The all-encompassing power of Ikhnaton's sun-god radiates from every line of his First Hymn, of which this is just a short extract;

> You made the distant sky in order to rise in it,
> In order to see all that you made
> While you were yet alone,
> Shining in your form as the living Aton,
> Dawning, glittering, travelling far and then returning . . .

Already the sun-god is seen as the creator-god, the first god who preceded all the visible forms on earth. In the neolithic, he must have been seen above all as the fructifying god who caused the earth to bring forth her harvest. Eulogies framed along these lines would have been sung or chanted at many sacred sites on the solstice apart from Stonehenge. In view of the Mount's function as an observatory for the solstices, that is an obvious place for a ritual celebration to welcome the sun-god's power into the Brookland basin.

During High Summer, the sun sets in the north-west. From this position, late afternoon and evening sunlight can shine obliquely and nostalgically onto the figure of the Wilmington Giant. Thus, at the time of the year when the sun shines with its fullest power, it illuminates its own personification to best effect. In its original state, with its outline one or two feet wide and a gleaming Chinese white, the portrait would have shown up startlingly against the dusky green of Windover Hill, while the barley on the surrounding hills and on the gentler chalk slopes below the figure grew tall and turned from green to gold.

The fulfilment of the sun-god's task came at the beginning of August, with a First Fruits feast at the Mount. Again, thanksgiving and rejoicing were the order of the day, no doubt with token offerings of produce being left on the Mount's summit platform. The rest of the harvest was gathered and, in September or October, the livestock fairs took place at Whitehawk and Combe Hill, which acted as separate regional centres. It seems likely that the boundary between their two territories was the River Ouse and that the Mount served *inter alia* as a meeting place for the two groups. The exchange of livestock and slaughter of surplus animals in the causewayed enclosures was the occasion of more feasting, this time of a wildly riotous character. The completion of the harvest and the prospect of a month or more of freedom from work gave additional cause for jubilation.

Then, after the autumn hunting forays into the Wealden forest, came the long period of waiting. These, the earliest farmers in Britain, needed reassurance that out of the chill depths of winter a new spring and a new summer would be born. The sun-gods of many successive cultures have been born in the middle of winter; Dionysus, Mithras and Attis were all born at the year's end. The solar year naturally ends as the sun's zenith reaches its lowest altitude and its life-giving power is spent. There can be no hiatus in the cosmic succession; therefore, as the sun-god dies so he is instantly reborn.

Celebration of the winter solstice, as the beginning of a new solar year, was psychologically essential. It was also of enormous practical importance to keep track of the calendar, so that crops could be sown at the right time. Even so, the winter was an anxious time, with adverse weather, food supplies gradually running down and the condition of byred livestock deteriorating. It was during this time that the figure of the guardian-god achieved its full significance as a reassuring reminder that the god would return, to pass down the Stonehenge Avenue and through the portal stones, to bring feasting and plenty again next summer.

THE COVENANT OF THE GUARDIAN-GOD

The guardian-god at Wilmington holds the dipylon firmly in his hands as he advances or perhaps even flies towards us. The gate-posts, both in fact and on the hill figure, served as a promise to the people he protected and fed in just the same way that the rainbow was offered by Jehovah to the people of Israel as a covenant that he would do them no hurt. Jehovah's covenant came immediately after the carnage of the Flood; so a sign of goodwill, albeit an ephemeral one, was certainly necessary. Here are the words of the Hebrew God, addressed to Noah:

> I establish my covenant with you, and with your seed after you, and with every living creature that is with you . . . neither shall all flesh be cut off any more by the waters of a flood; neither shall there any more be a flood to destroy the earth. This is the token of the covenant which I make between me and you and every living creature that is with you, for perpetual generations: I do set my bow in the cloud and it shall be for a token of a covenant between me and the earth. When I bring a cloud over the earth, the bow shall be seen in the cloud: and I will remember my covenant . . . and I will look upon it, that I may remember the everlasting covenant.

(Genesis 9:9-16)

The Hebrew God was to remind himself of his promise by producing a rainbow. The neolithic Guardian was reminded by his people that he was duty bound, in exchange for offerings, sacrifices, prayers, praise, songs, loyalty and who knows what else, to return each summer to kindle the crops. He was reminded by being shown a huge portrait of himself standing between the ceremonial gate-posts. It was a double-sided cipher. It served to remind the Guardian in the sky of his guardianship over man; it served also to remind man that his faith in the Guardian would not be betrayed.

THE SHORT REIGN OF JOHN BARLEYCORN

The sun-god's direct involvement in man's affairs may have been short; it was probably seen, in ritual terms, as the period between May Day or the summer solstice and the First Fruits feast. The brevity of this reign, at most three months long, is reflected in later fertility cults in which the earth-goddess, who is immortal, is impregnated annually by a short-lived consort. There is a distant echo of the sun-god as a mercurial lover, doomed to die at the end of each summer, in John Barleycorn. John Barleycorn is the barley-god who has his day at harvest time but must die at the completion of the harvest. In the form of a corn idol, or 'dolly', he was frequently buried, or in other words ritually murdered, during the ploughing that followed the harvest. And so the cycle could be repeated; with his death, John Barleycorn ensured fertility for the following year's crops. The neolithic myth is still re-enacted in song at Haxey in Lincolnshire on Plough Monday (6 January):

> There was three men came out of the west,
> Their fortunes for to try,
> And these three men made a solemn vow,
> John Barleycorn should die.
> They ploughed, they sowed, they harrowed him in,
> Throwed clods upon his head,
> And three men made a solemn vow,
> John Barleycorn was dead.

The corn dolly is generally taken, both by folklorists and by contemporary rural traditions, to represent the earth-goddess, the Great or Mother Goddess whose cults permeated neolithic and Bronze Age civilizations. This may be mistaken, in view of the John Barleycorn myth and in view of the ancient traditions of slaying the queen's male consort in order to ensure prosperity and fertility for the following year. Robert Graves (1948 and 1960) makes much of the matrilineal societies of Bronze Age Greece and explains that it was a ritual necessity to sacrifice the consort as the sun's power declined towards the close of each year. The male consort's death was essential to produce the next harvest. Only as the consort acquired priestly or administrative duties was the practice ended so that he might continue as king, and even then an annual mock death was required in the form of a token abdication, usually accompanied by the sacrifice of a surrogate-king or *interrex*.

The long ancestry of the corn dolly, made anew every year to be destroyed every year, can thus be traced back to the annual sacrifice of the queen's consort. This ritual, too, is a piece of sympathetic magic, performed in the hope that the earth-goddess would also be made fecund by her ephemeral consort, the sun-god, who would then wane in power ready for the next agricultural cycle.

It is clear that although names may differ from region to region and from century to century, there is a coherent tradition in which a seasonal appearance is made by an impregnating visitor. He is John Barleycorn, the Green Man, Jack-in-Green, the Midsummer Giant; it is a short step to see the same figure in the Wilmington

Giant, the Long Man or the Green Man of Wilmington.

It is tempting to set East Sussex apart as a separate mythogenetic region from the rest of neolithic Europe, if only because there is currently such a strong literary tradition that the Great Goddess cult was supreme during the neolithic. But this is not entirely borne out by the evidence. Ritual gate-posts or portals that are clearly designed to guide or salute the power of the sun are to be found elsewhere than in East Sussex. The Stonehenge portal stones have been mentioned already; other stone circles and stone rows as far afield as Aberdeen have them too. It is also clear from artefacts found at neolithic and Bronze Age sites that the importance of the male role in fertilization was well understood. Great emphasis has been placed on the earth-goddess figurines; but just as many chalk or bone phalli have been found at English sites, showing that the male principle was held in some awe and that the sexual interaction between male and female principles on a cosmic level was also appreciated. In one of the flint mines at Grimes Graves in Norfolk a small altar was found. It was a simple affair, consisting of a conical mound of flints surmounted by seven antler tines, the tools used for quarrying the flints, and a small chalk libation-cup. On the wall behind the little pyramid was a ledge carrying a 'fat lady' statuette of the Earth Mother, carved in chalk, and a chalk phallus.

The Great Goddess, the supreme Earth Mother, was the enduring and immortal presence in the neolithic consciousness. We have only to think of the very rich neolithic culture of Malta, dating back to about 3500 BC, and which produced numerous 'fat lady' figurines. Both seated and standing representations of the goddess were found at the great neolithic temple at Hagar Qim. It was in a niche at the underground temple or Hypogeum at Hal Saflieni that the famous 'Sleeping Lady' figurine was discovered. Some of the statuettes are headless and cord-holes in the throat show that the heads were made separately, possibly so that they could be made to nod. The most impressive representation of the Mother Goddess is the gigantic but sadly mutilated figure in the south temple at Tarxien. It is broken off at waist level yet, even in this condition, it is a powerful presence, dominating the temple. When complete, the Tarxien goddess would have stood an imposing nine feet high. Quite apart from showing the great importance of the goddess, this gives us further proof that in 2400 BC the neolithic spirit was capable of conceiving colossal representations of deities.

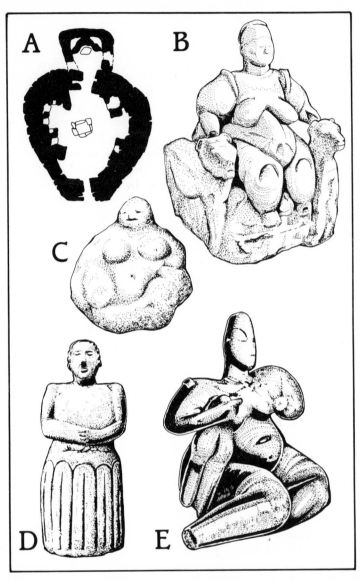

Figure 26. The neolithic earth-mother goddess. A: Hut No. 8 at Skara Brae, Orkney, may incorporate a homage to the goddess in its plan, *c*.2500 BC. B. goddess giving birth on a leopard throne, Çatal Hüyük, Turkey, *c*.5000 BC. C: chalk figurine of the goddess from a flint mine at Grimes' Graves, Norfolk, *c*.2500 BC. D: goddess with child from Haçilar, Turkey, *c*.5000 BC. E: goddess figurine from Tarxien temple, Malta, *c*.2000 BC.

It is possible that certain buildings intended for ritual purposes incorporated the stylized image of the Great Goddess in their plans. The arrangement of several Maltese temples, with two pairs of transepts and an apse, suggests an anthropoidal form with arms, legs and head. At the neolithic stone village of Skara Brae in Orkney, *one* hut (Hut No. 8) has a distinctly human form, although it could be interpreted as male or female. The long axis of this hut lies due north-south, so it may, like the Long Man, be intended to honour the sun-god; but interpretation is very uncertain.

Either way, the central position of the Earth Mother is not disputed. What has been overlooked by other writers is the ephemeral visitations of the sun-god or barley-god or guardian-god, whose vital role in the propagation and sustenance of life was fully appreciated by neolithic man. A poem from the threshold of the neolithic gives a clue to the strange, ambivalent attitude to the male principle. It comes from a tomb in the Sumerian city of Ur, dating from about 2000 BC, and speaks of five kings of Ur as if each one was a separate manifestation of Damu, the ever-living, ever-dying god of Sumer.

The Sumerian equivalent of the Great Goddess was Inanna. Damu and Inanna, Tammuz and Ishtar, Adonis and Aphrodite, Osiris and Isis: in each early culture, female was paired with male, even if only an ephemeral male. So it was in neolithic Sussex, except that the names of the god and goddess are unknown; but the mercurial guardian-god and the earth-goddess were both essential to the myth.

THE NECESSITY OF MYTH

Why was there a need for a myth, and so absorbing and monumental a myth as the one that evolved in neolithic England? Part of the answer lies in the three aspirations of man as seen in classical Indian philosophy: love, power and order. In a small social group, such as the palaeolithic hunting band, it is just possible for all three needs to be met. But with the advent of farming, craft industries and sedentary communities, social groups inevitably became larger and more differentiated. In this situation, the three aspirations — especially order — would tend to be more difficult to satisfy. Power needed some external foundation if inequalities in society were to be maintained, rationalized and enforced without the system becoming oppressive, which is the modern solution to the problem.

It was under these pressures that astronomy was 'discovered' or perhaps, in the context of the present discussion, invented. Even primitive cosmogonies reveal order and harmony in the universe and, indeed, astronomy and cosmology were devised, consciously or unconsciously, in order to do so. The cosmos itself provided an orderly context for the microcosm of social order and helped to reconcile the three unbalanced interest systems. Astronomy also created a fourth area of endeavour: the apprehension of the mystery of the universe. Whether the universe was properly understood in any scientific or systematic sense does not matter; even if it is based on a very partial understanding or total misunderstanding, awe by itself can be immensely satisfying, transcending the winds of everyday passions. Indeed, standing today on Windover Hill or in front of the Giant or on the Mount, and seeing the world as neolithic man saw it, even modern man, shackled as he is by a scientific-materialist background, can experience what Joyce called 'the luminous silent stasis of aesthetic pleasure'.

Awe before the partly apprehended mystery of the world is now fully developed only in oriental meditation religions, but it is a state that was developed to some degree in neolithic Britain. Neolithic man was intoxicated with his new vision of the universe, and it could be argued that he over-reacted to it. The artefacts he designed and crafted to help him relate to the universe and to express that relationship have long outlasted his civilization. His monuments to time and to the passage of time have long outlived his race. His cenotaphs to death and renewal have endured beyond any coherent folk-memory that could elucidate them in detail.

Was it all a tragic miscalculation, like the colossal statue of Ozymandias that lies wrecked in the desert in Shelley's poem? Were the circles, henges, barrows and the Long Man himself *too* durable, built as they were in the fervour of revelation? It may be so, but it is also true that neolithic man had unusual breadth of vision and thought in unusually long spans of time. It is possible that he was reconciled or resigned to seeing his culture subtly, gradually transformed with time until the garbling of oral traditions rendered it unrecognizable: but yet wanted to be sure that some timeless and indestructible ciphers survived, not only as reminders but as keys to the enduring values.

If this view is correct, we can risk making clumsy mistakes in our attempts to decipher the remains that are left to us, and we must risk appearing over-zealous in our insistence that not a single neolithic monument should be allowed to suffer damage. How much neolithic man drew from all this cosmological activity can only be surmised. At one end of the scale, it may have been no more than a cigarette in a tea-break, a fleeting moment of escape from everyday drudgery. At the other end of the scale, the entire farming community may have been 'high' on mystical revelation. It is probable, in view of the small size of the communities and the ambitious scale of most of their religous structures, that their experience of the numinous was fairly continuous.

The neolithic mythology, like any other mythology with real spiritual and psychological power, contained the great polarities of human experience: male and female, birth and death, growth and decay, youth and age, happiness and sorrow. Mythic power is engendered by the interaction of opposites, in just the same way that opposing electrical charges in a thunder cloud generate lightning. By generating mythic power, man becomes at once the begetter and the potential destroyer of the gods. This was one of the great, dark, powerful secrets of the neolithic.

The talismanic portrait of the guardian-god at Wilmington symbolized a contract between man and his guardian. That covenant made man at once the slave and the master of his god. It is not at all likely that he thought of the relationship in these terms, yet it helps us to express it in this way so that we can see how it was that he felt confident in his relationship with the universe as a whole.

There was, as a result of this confidence, a comfortable family feeling in the neolithic cosmogony, with earth as mother, sun as father and man as their brood of loyal and dutiful children. But what exactly was the nature of the sun-god? How far can the spare outline of the Long Man be filled out with telling details of character, appearance and biography? Obviously there are no written accounts of any sort surviving from the neolithic: at least nothing survives that we recognize as writing in the modern sense. The curiously scratched tablets from Whitehawk and the Trundle, as well as other examples such as the large collection of ideographs at the Abri Leuillet near Paris, cannot be translated in the way that ancient Egyptian hieroglyphs can, even though a rudimentary vocabulary of nature concepts can be discerned in some of them. In a great deal of neolithic art, it is difficult to distinguish between stylized representations of objects, expressions of concepts, or purely abstract decorations.

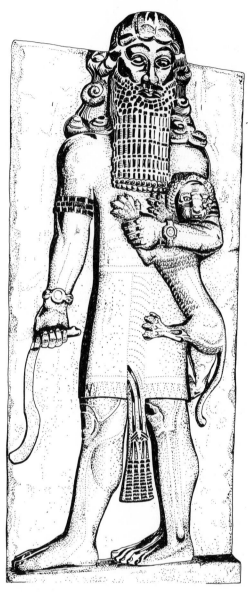

Figure 27. Gilgamesh. A colossal statue from Khorsabad, Iraq, *c*.1000 BC. The Sumerian sun-hero carries a lion as an emblem of the sun-god: the sickle confirms that he is a fertility figure. Gilgamesh was a direct descendant of the neolithic sun-god and an ancestor of the biblical Samson.

LATE SURVIVALS OF THE NEOLITHIC SUN-GOD

The chances of finding out much more about the sun-god from original neolithic sources, then, do not appear to be very good. There are, nevertheless, secondary sources that are useful, provided they are treated with due caution. It is important to remember that later cultures grew out of the neolithic and, although technologies, beliefs and customs changed during the Bronze and Iron Ages, substantial vestiges of the Old Ways will have survived. The survival of John Barleycorn and Maypole dancing into the twentieth century proves how persistent ancient beliefs and customs can be.

Two important qualities of the sun-god that survived into the Iron Age are phenomenal strength and courageous self-sacrifice. Jung and Steinthal both interpret the Samson of scripture as a survival of an older sun-god. Samson kills a lion with his bare hands. Although Samson is the sun-god, the lion too is a symbol of the fierce heat of the sun in midsummer. When Samson struggles with the lion, he struggles with himself; when he kills it, he kills himself with his own hands. The theme is more explicit still at the well-known end of the story when, blinded and in chains, Samson destroys himself by pulling the roof down on his own head. The Phoenicians and Assyrians similarly believed that their sun-god was committing annual suicide; it was the only way in which they could explain the conundrum of absolute power submitting to enfeeblement.

The sun-god or sun-hero is typically a young man, extremely good-looking, with glowing hair and sometimes a fiery crown. In addition to his youth, courage, vigour, fiery impetuosity and his reputation as a conqueror, he possesses the mature quality of judgement: he is a god to be trusted absolutely, as well as a god to love and admire. The Roman Mithras, who was a sun-hero, was referred to as 'the well-beloved'. The hymn of St Ambrose inadvertently addresses Christ as a sun-hero: 'O sol salutis'; Melito in his turn called him 'the sun of the East'.

Thus, the character of the neolithic sun-god has survived even within the purlieus of Christianity. St John Chrysostom, in his treatise *De solstitiis et aequinoctiis*, was very conscious of the aptness of these solar references to Christology, and saw how close Christ was to the long tradition of Near Eastern sun-heroes;

But the Lord, too, was born in wintertime, on the twenty-fifth of

December, when the ripe olives are pressed in order to produce the oil for anointing, the chrism. They also call this day the birthday of the Unconquerable One [Mithras]. Yet who is as unconquerable as our lord, who overthrew and conquered death itself? He himself is the sun of right-eousness of whom the prophet Malachi spoke. He is the lord of light and darkness.

So the solstitial birth of Christ itself gives us a biographical detail accorded to sun-heroes in general. There is some archaeological evidence for believing that the birth or renewal of the neolithic and Bronze Age sun-god was celebrated on the winter solstice. The principal hut in the Bronze Age farmstead on Itford Hill had an entrance porch oriented to the south-east, which is the direction of the sunrise in midwinter. The planting of the votive phallus close to the doorway may have been intended as a ritual conception, a piece of sympathetic magic to induce the rebirth of the sun-god. The orientation of the door, as the means by which the welcome visitor enters the dwelling, is a feature likely to have been given some consideration in an age when directions of cosmic visitations were highly significant.

Similarly, the main entrance through the ditch and bank at Durrington Walls was oriented towards the south-east. Immed-iately inside the gap in the bank stood the great Southern Rotunda, with its doorway and its huge dipylon also oriented towards the mid-winter sunrise. Was there, perhaps, a feast to celebrate the sun-god's birth on the winter solstice, a remote precursor of Christmas?

An aspect of the sun-god's biography that has been touched on repeatedly is his travelling. His daily passage across the sky was observable proof that he was on a journey. The night journey was wrapped in mystery. Since the world disc was assumed to be edged by ocean, the sun's daily journey clearly ended by plunging into the ocean. In some mythologies, the sun-god or sun-hero travels by ship and is then swallowed by a sea monster. He fights it from within or kindles a fire and eventually re-emerges. The vicissitudes of the hero during his night sea journey recur in culture after culture, from the Polynesian myth of Rata to Longfellow's Hiawatha. As Hiawatha prepares for his journey to the Western Land, he says,

> 'I am going, O Nokomis,
> On a long and distant journey,
> To the portals of the sunset . . .'
> Thus departed Hiawatha,

Hiawatha the Beloved,
In the glory of the sunset,
In the purple mists of evening,
To the regions of the homewind.

It is curious that, even in this very late re-working of the sun-god myth, Longfellow refers to his hero as 'the Beloved'. It seems to be almost universal for the sun-god or sun-hero to inspire nostalgic longing and an indefinable affection. We have only to think of the weeping for the deaths of Tammuz and Baldur, of Venus' sadness at the death of Adonis, as described by Shakespeare;

She looks upon his lips, and they are pale;
She takes him by the hand, and that is cold;
She whispers in his ears a heavy tale,
As if they heard the woeful words she told:
She lifts the coffer-lids that close his eyes,
Where lo! two lamps, burnt out, in darkness lies:

Two glasses where herself herself beheld
A thousand times, and now no more reflect;
Their virtue lost, wherein they late excell'd,
And every beauty robb'd of his effect:
'Wonder of time,' quoth she, 'this is my spite,
That you being dead the day should yet be light.'

But these expressions of sentiment are associated with the decline and departure of the god-hero. In the perihelion of his power, his character appears totally different from the moist-eyed wistfulness of sunset and autumn. The god's midday or midsummer aspect is fierce, forceful and courageous, the most dynamic and concentrated symbol of life force imaginable. The sun has always symbolized libido, both in the limited sense of the carnal wish and in the more general sense of mental and emotional vitality. It is therefore entirely natural that the sun has occasionally been depicted with a phallus or even with several phalli, turning the image into a spoked but rimless wheel.

It is this image of the sun-god, fertile, beneficent and tense with power and authority, that stands on the hillside at Wilmington. But the Windover Phallus, which belongs to the Giant, is clearly not to be taken too literally; the Long Mound is 260 feet long, which is 20 feet longer than the Giant. It also stands separately, above the figure. The Windover Phallus is to be seen instead as a symbol of the god's role as Bringer of Life, and the fact that it points directly at

Plate 8. Odin, 'All-Father'. The Norse version of the guardian-god in his mature, powerful, high-summer aspect. Like the old neolithic god, he sacrifices himself to ensure nature's continuity: 'I hung on the windy tree for nine full nights; I was wounded with spear and offered to Odin, myself to myself.'

the head of the hill figure shows that it rules his mental processes. Although it is phallic, it should be taken, like the dipylon, as part of the god's insignia, and thus as part of the neolithic concept of the god and his works. The strange 'pillar' altars found in Maltese temples such as Hagar Qim may be a reference to the same complex of ideas.

EUROPEAN ANTECEDENTS OF THE GUARDIAN-GOD

If the Giant has successors in the later and better-known mythologies of Europe, he also has ancestors there. The neolithic age began earlier on the mainland of Europe than in Britain, so it should not be surprising to find statuettes of a male deity dating back to 5000 BC. Striking among these are the standing, ithyphallic figures, some of which wear horned animal masks; they are clearly related to fertility rituals. More significant still is the 'sickle-god' found at Szegvár in south-east Hungary and now in the Koszlá József Museum in Szentes. This 10-inch-high figurine shows a regal, seated male figure. His arms are bent so that his hands rest on his chest. His right hand holds a sickle which curves over his right shoulder. He wears a flat mask, arm rings on both wrists and a waist-band with a zig-zag pattern. The sickle-god is a dignified and authoritative figure, supervising the barley harvest from his throne. The inference is plain. The Wilmington Giant is the solstitial aspect of the god, arriving to begin the High Summer season; the sickle-god is the First Fruits aspect of the god. They are one and the same god, in June and August.

The changing aspect of the guardian-god during the year has led some to call him the year-god. The multiplicity of names should not be allowed to confuse the issue; year-god, guardian-god, barley-god, sickle-god and sun-god are all the same, single deity. Professor Gimbutas (1974) points out that Dionysus, although much later, is really the same deity as well. Robert Graves (1960) mentions that Dionysus' association with wine is a late superimposition on his original role as beer-god, which links him neatly with John Barleycorn.

The neolithic year-god or sun-god on mainland Europe had a life cycle that spanned a year, just like the sun-gods of later myths. He began as the Divine Child, the infant born at the winter solstice, and grew into the midsummer guardian-god, a strong creator-king who came into his own during High Summer. Then, necessarily, came the season of decline. The autumn aspect of the god was peaceful,

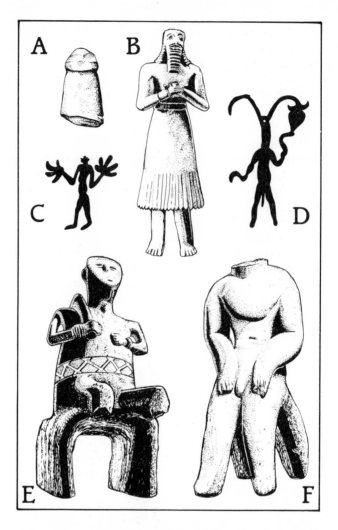

Figure 28. The neolithic guardian-god. A: bone phallus from The Trundle. B: the Lord of Life, a Sumerian cult statue from Tell Asmar, *c*.3000 BC; the cup signifies the feast following the annual wedding of the god and goddess. C: rock engraving at Bacinete, Spain, *c*.3000 BC; sun-ray fingers show that he is the sun-god. D: rock engraving at Cueva de los Letreros, Spain, *c*.3000 BC; horns, fruit and sickles are emblems of the fertility god. E: enthroned sickle-god from Szegvár-Tüzköves, Hungary, 5000 BC; supervising the harvest, he is the high-summer aspect of the god of the early neolithic. F: enthroned god from Pyrasos, Thessaly, 5500 BC.

thoughtful, ageing, resigned. Solid evidence of this third aspect again comes from eastern Europe. A figurine called 'The Thinker' was found at Cernavoda in eastern Romania; another, called 'The Sorrowful God' was found at Tirpesti. 'The Thinker' is dated to around 5000 BC and 'The Sorrowful God' to about 4500 BC. Both show the sun-god in a squatting position with his knees drawn up to his chest. They show him sapped of vitality, lethargic, contemplative.

It is possible to see a large analogue of 'The Sorrowful God' in the living landscape of the East Sussex downs: an even huger representation of the god than the Wilmington Giant. Time and again the peculiar form of the South Downs has evoked analogies with organic forms. There is Gilbert White's famous description of the 'gentle swellings and smooth fungus-like protuberances' of the downs, with their 'air of vegetative dilatation' (Letter 56). W. H. Hudson (1942) went further, in comparing the hills with gigantic human forms: 'the succession of shapely outlines, the vast protuberances and deep divisions between, suggestive of the most

Figure 29. The 'Thinker' or 'Sorrowful God' of Cernavoda, Romania, c.5000 BC. The nearest modern approximation to the aged aspect of the year-god is the senile, but still benevolent, Father Christmas.

prominent and beautiful curves of the human figure . . . a Titanic woman reclined in everlasting slumber on the earth, her loose sweet-smelling hair lying like an old-world forest over leagues of ground; the poet himself sitting for ever, immersed in melancholy, in the shadow of her great head.' As Hudson himself said, the picture may seem to be the outcome of mere morbidity, a literary device only; but when Windover Hill is seen from the south-west it returns to the mind in a new light entirely.

Hindover Hill was mentioned in Chapter 8 as the possible site of a defaced long barrow and it also has intervisibility lines with long barrows at Charlston and Windover. From the Bronze Dial at Hindover, there is a superb view north-east towards Windover. From this viewpoint, Tenantry Ground looks like the bowed head of a gigantic, exhausted figure, Wilmington Hill like the slightly raised left shoulder, the spur leading south-south-west from Wilmington Hill the left arm and the spur from Windover to Lullington Church the right arm. Windover Hill then becomes the nape of an enormous squatting figure, with its arms thrown forward and its head slumped lifelessly on its chest. Seen in this way, the figure is only partial. The Giant is tattooed on its back and the lower half of the sunken, defeated body has been subsumed into the earth. It is a colossal realization of the autumnal decline of the guardian-god, the demise of John Barleycorn. His short reign over, the barley-god submits to reincorporation into the fabric of Mother Earth.

'A GOD OF ENORMOUS POWER, WITH A SHINING COUNTENANCE'
If the mercurial sun-god of the neolithic has been neglected in modern times, it may be that he was overlooked because he was so conspicuous. Like his portrait on Windover Hill, he has been lost beneath the green carpet of thyme, physically overwhelmed by the rich variety of organisms that he has helped to create, historically overtaken by the evolution of more elaborate mythologies that nevertheless have him as their starting point.

'The path of the visible gods will appear through the disc of the sun, who is God my father,' said Mithras, according to the Mithraic liturgy. And it is from Mithraic liturgy that one of the most evocative descriptions of the midsummer sun-god comes. It may be that the details are anachronistic in relation to the neolithic god, but the spirit of the description has an authentic, archetypal ring:

You will see a god of enormous power, with a shining countenance, young, with golden hair, in a white tunic and golden crown . . . You will see lightning leap from his eyes and from his body, stars.

Still more vivid, because more abstract and therefore more timeless, is the Third Prayer of the liturgy. After the Second Prayer, the neophyte is engulfed by five-pointed stars that float down from the sun in great numbers: then he sees the closed, flaming doors on the sun's disc. After this, he speaks the Third Prayer:

Listen to me, Lord, you who have fastened the fiery bolts of heaven, double-bodied, fire-ruler, creator of light, fire-breathing, fiery-hearted, shining spirit, rejoicing in fire, beautiful light, Lord of light, giver of light, sower of fire, confounding with fire, living light, whirling fire, moving light, hurler of thunderbolts, conqueror of the stars.

The extravagance and exuberance of this outpouring brings us close to the exaltation of the neolithic religious spirit, even though it was written two thousand years after the neolithic melted imperceptibly into the Bronze Age. The Mithraic effusion corresponds, in time only, to the handful of dull and lustreless sherds which mark the soil covering the guardian-god: the Roman sherds that rest halfway between the buried figure of the god and the sunlit world that is his kingdom. Yet the sherds and the covering soil are a salutary reminder that the god was first celebrated and later neglected: that in the stratigraphy of the figure there may be further evidence of its date.

At present only tentative and provisional dates can be offered. If we assume, for the moment, that Whitehawk, Combe Hill, the Windover Long Mound, the flint mines and the Mount were all contemporary with the Giant, there is still a wide time window that can accommodate all these, beginning in 4000 BC and ending in 2500 BC. Imprecise though this is, it means that the hill figure is five or six thousand years old.

Without firm radiocarbon dates, we can only arrive at inferential dates for the neolithic sites of East Sussex based on comparison with dated sites elsewhere. Whitehawk is culturally very close to Windmill Hill, so it is logical to attribute the same date, about 3400 BC, although the enclosure probably continued in use for several centuries after its foundation. The Mount, as a smaller, less ambitious version of the Silbury harvest hill, was probably built earlier than the 2800 BC date attributed to Silbury. The use of the

Brookland basin as a large celestial clock is related to the concepts underlying the design of Stonehenge I. Because more landscape was used than artifice, and because only the relatively simple solar observations were made at the Mount, we can place it significantly earlier than 2900 BC, the date of the Stonehenge I ditch. Since the Mount is linked physically to Whitehawk by Juggs' Road, it was probably contemporary with Whitehawk or only slightly later, perhaps about 3300 BC.

The Windover Long Mound, with its unique and evolved phallic form, is likely to be late by comparison with other long barrows, so that a date of about 3200 BC, in the centre of the middle neolithic, is most probable. Since the long axis of the Windover Phallus is aligned with the Giant's head, it is almost certain that the Giant was constructed first, and that the Long Mound and Cursus were made immediately afterwards. So the circumstantial evidence argues for a middle neolithic date, around 3200 BC, as the most favourable for the creation of the Wilmington Giant.

Nameless though he must probably remain for ever, his attributes are now known at least in part. He was the phallic, fertilizing god whose annual visitations ensured that life would be renewed, the transient but glorious consort of the Great Goddess, the guardian of the harvests and, above all else, the bringer of feast and plenty to his people. At last, the great icon inscribed on the side of Windover Hill has yielded up its principal mystery. At last we know who the Giant is and why he was drawn there. It may eventually be possible to disentangle the other, deceptively simple, ideographs from the neolithic and piece together still more of its beliefs and myths. But even if no more is ever learned, this one icon with its concentrated, hieratic and reductive message tells of an important and unsuspected dimension to neolithic mythology in England. For the Wilmington Giant now stands revealed as the oldest known god of these islands.

*   *   *

APPENDIX I
STATISTICAL TREATMENTS OF NEOLITHIC SITES IN SUSSEX

It is clear from any map showing the distribution of neolithic sites in Sussex that a certain amount of clustering exists. There is, for example, a focus of activity in the Trundle-Bevis's Thumb area of West Sussex and another in the Windover Hill area of East Sussex. In order to subject this qualitative observation to an objective test, a nearest neighbour analysis was run on the distribution.

Nearest neighbour analysis is relatively straightforward and relates the nearness-to-nearest-neighbour for all the neolithic sites to the area of the South Downs. An index of 0.0 would show that the sites were entirely clustered; an index of 1.0 would show completely random dispersion. The neolithic sites of the South Downs yield an index of 0.12, which tells us that they are very clustered indeed.

The significance of the clustering is underlined by the results of a second statistical test. By calculating the mean of the map co-ordinates of the sites, we can find the mean centre of the distribution, i.e. its 'centre of gravity'. Once this is found, the distance of each individual site from the mean centre can be measured, and then the mean distance from the mean centre calculated. The results are as follows:

Site-distribution	O.S. Grid Reference of Mean Centre	Mean Distance from Mean Centre
West Sussex	830114	2.1 miles
East Sussex	491040	4.1 miles
South Downs	258065	18.2 miles

The low figures of two miles and four miles for mean distance in the two halves of the South Downs prove a high degree of clustering within those two areas and strong focusing on the two mean centres. This clustering is emphasized by comparison with the mean distance for the South Downs as a whole: a much higher figure than would have been expected from a combination of the two component distributions if they had been randomly dispersed internally (see Figure 14).

The tests prove that the neolithic sites of the South Downs resolve into two separate geographical clusters: one in West Sussex, the other in East Sussex. The East Sussex cluster has its mean centre close to the halfway point between Long Burgh and the Giant's Grave.

APPENDIX II
A CHRONOLOGICAL TABLE OF BRITISH HILL FIGURES

Wilmington Giant	Sussex	Neolithic	ED 1766
Cerne Giant	Dorset	Iron Age?	ED 1764?
Gog and Magog (dest.)	Cambridge	Iron Age?	ED 1605
Shotover Giant (dest.)	Oxford	?	ED 1640
Gogmagog & Corineus (dest.)	Plymouth	Iron Age?	ED 1486
Uffington White Horse	Berkshire	Iron Age?	ED 1486
Red Horse of Tysoe (dest.)	Warwickshire	Saxon?	ED 1607
Whiteleaf Cross	Bucks	Medieval	ED 1742
Bledlow Cross	Bucks	Medieval	ED 1827
Ditchling Cross	Sussex	Medieval	ED 1901?
Westbury (Bratton) Horse I	Wilts	1700	
Watlington White Mark	Bucks	1764	
Mermond Horse & Stag	Aberdeen	1775	
Westbury Horse II	Wilts	1778	
Oldbury (Cherhill) Horse	Wilts	1780	
Pewsey Horse I	Wilts	1785	
Marlborough Horse	Wilts	1804	
Alton Barnes Horse	Wilts	1812	
Osmington Horse	Dorset	1815?	
Hackpen Horse	Wilts	1838	
Hindover (Litlington) Horse I	Sussex	1838	
Devizes Horse (dest.)	Wilts	1845	
Kilburn Horse	Yorks	1857	
Woolborough Horse	Hants	1860	
Broad Town Horse	Wilts	1863	
Ham Hill Horse (dest.)	Wilts	1865	
Wye Royal Crown	Kent	1902	
Aeroplane, Dover	Kent	1909	
Fovant Down Badges (14)	Wilts	1914-18	
Bulford Kiwi	Wilts	1918	
Hindover Horse II	Sussex	1924	
Whipsnade Lion	Bucks	1933	
Pewsey Horse II	Wilts	1937	

ED = Earliest known documentary evidence.

Principal source: *White Horses and Other Hill Figures* by Morris Marples, Country Life Books (1949).

REFERENCES

Abbreviations: *Sussex Archaeological Collection — SAC.*
Sussex County Magazine — SCM.

Chapter 1: Beginnings
Anon. (1939) 'The Damage to the Long Man', *SCM* 13, 431.
Beckett, A. (1909) *The Spirit of the Downs*, Methuen.
Furneaux, R. (1976) *Ancient Mysteries*, White Lion.
Heron-Allen, E. (1939) 'The Long Man of Wilmington and its Roman Origin', *SCM* 13, 655-660.
Hudson, W. H. (1942) *Nature in Downland*, Dent.
Jung, C. G. (1956) *Symbols of Transformation* (trans. Hull), Routledge and Kegan Paul.
Sidgwick, J. B. (1939) 'The Mystery of the Long Man', *SCM* 13, 408-420.

Chapter 2: The Giant Described
Cooper, G. M. (1851) 'Wilmington Priory and Church', *SAC* 4, 37-63.
Gerster, G. (1976) *Grand Design*, Paddington Press.
Holden, E. W. (1971) 'Some Notes on the Long Man of Wilmington', *SAC* 109, 37-54.
Horsfield, T. W. (1835) *History of Sussex*.
Phené, J. S. (1872) 'Results of a Recent Investigation into Ancient Monuments and Relics', *Trans. Roy. Inst. of Brit. Architects* 3, 181.

Pyatt, E. C. (1972) *Chalkways of South and South-east England*, David and Charles.

St Croix, W. de (1881) 'The Wilmington Giant', *SAC* 26, 97-112.

Wildman, S. G. (1971) *The Black Horsemen: English Inns and King Arthur*, John Baker.

Chapter 3: The Quest

Annett, S. F. (1932) 'The "Long Man" of Wilmington', *SCM* 6, 402-404.

Cooper, G. M. (1851) 'Wilmington Priory and Church', *SAC* 4, 37-63.

Crow, W. B. (1968) *A History of Magic, Witchcraft and Occultism*, Aquarian Press.

Godfrey, W. H. (1928) 'Wilmington Priory: An Architectural Description', *SAC* 69, 1-52.

Rhodes, H. T. F. (1954) *The Satanic Mass*, Rider.

Senior, M. (1979) *Myths of Britain*, Orbis.

Sidgwick, J. B. (1939) 'The Mystery of the Long Man', *SCM* 13, 408-420.

Chapter 4: Saxon Kings and Saxon Gods

Brandon, P. (1978) *The South Saxons*, Phillimore.

Branston, B. (1974) *The Lost Gods of England*, Thames and Hudson (2nd ed.).

Bulfinch, T. (1915) *The Golden Age of Myth and Legend*, Harrap.

Chrétien de Troyes (1914) *Arthurian Romances*, Dent-Everyman.

Ellis Davidson, H. R. (1969) *Scandinavian Mythology*, Hamlyn.

Holden, E. W. (1971) 'Some Notes on the Long Man of Wilmington', *SAC* 109, 37-54.

Page, R. I. (1970) *Life in Anglo-Saxon England*, Batsford.

Sawyer, F. E. (1891) 'S. Wilfrith's Life in Sussex and the Introduction of Christianity', *SAC* 33, 101-128.

Sidgwick, J. B. (1939) 'The Mystery of the Long Man', *SCM* 13, 408-420.

Chapter 5: Veni, Vidi

Gibbon, E. (1914) *Decline and Fall of the Roman Empire* (ed. J. B. Bury).

Heron-Allen, E. (1939) 'The Long Man of Wilmington and its Roman Origin', *SCM* 13, 655-660.

Holden, E. W. (1971) 'Some Notes on the Long Man of Wilmington', SAC 109, 37-54.

Kagan, D. (1962) *Decline and Fall of the Roman Empire*, Heath.
Margary, I. D. (1965) *Roman Ways in the Weald*, Phoenix House.
Passmore, A. D. (1937) *Sussex Notes and Queries* 6, 252.

Chapter 6: The Fires of Sacrifice

Crow, W. B. (1968) *A History of Magic, Witchcraft and Occultism*, Aquarian Press.
Dyer, J. (1973) *Southern England: An Archaeological Guide*, Faber and Faber.
Harding, D. W. (1978) *Prehistoric Europe*, Elsevier-Phaidon.
Laing, L. (1979) *Celtic Britain*, Routledge and Kegan Paul.
St Croix, W. de (1881) 'The Wilmington Giant', *SAC* 26, 97-112.
Senior, M. (1979) *Myths of Britain*, Orbis.

Chapter 7: The Kingdom of the Sun

Balfour, M. (1979) *Stonehenge and its Mysteries*, Macdonald and Jane's.
Branston, B. (1974) *The Lost Gods of England*, Thames and Hudson.
Bratton, F. G. (1961) *The Heretic Pharaoh*, Robert Hale.
Curwen, E. C. (1928) 'The Antiquities of Windover Hill', *SAC* 69, 93-101.
Dyer, J. (1973) *Southern England: An Archaeological Guide*, Faber and Faber.
Ellis Davidson, H. R. (1969) *Scandinavian Mythology*, Hamlyn.
Field, L. F. (1939) 'Castle Hill, Newhaven', *SAC* 80, 263-292.
Grinsell, L. V. (1931) 'Sussex in the Bronze Age', *SAC* 72, 30-68.
Lemesurier, P. (1977) *The Great Pyramid Decoded*, Compton Russell.
Michell, J. (1973) *The View Over Atlantis*, Abacus.
O'Connor, T. P. (1976) 'The Excavation of a Round Barrow and Cross-Ridge Dyke at Alfriston, East Sussex, 1975', *SAC* 114, 151-163.
Petrie, W. F. (1926) 'The Hill Figures of England', *Roy. Anthrop. Inst. Occasional Papers*, 7.
Sidgwick, J. B. (1939) 'The Mystery of the Long Man', *SCM* 13, 408-420.
Smyth, C. P. (1880) *Our Inheritance in the Great Pyramid*, Isbister.
Sykes, E. (1952) *Dictionary of Non-Classical Mythology*, Dent.

Chapter 8: Death Rites and Eternity

Burl, A. (1976) *The Stone Circles of the British Isles*, Yale University Press.

Curwen, E. C. (1928) 'The Antiquities of Windover Hill', *SAC* 69, 93-101.

Curwen, E. C. (1934) *The Archaeology of Sussex*, Methuen.

Dames, M. (1977) *The Avebury Cycle,* Thames and Hudson.

Drewett, P. (1975) 'The Excavation of an Oval Burial Mound . . . at Alfriston, East Sussex', *Proc. Prehist. Soc.* 41, 119-152.

Gimbutas, M. (1974) *The Gods and Goddesses of Old Europe, 7000-3500 BC*, Thames and Hudson.

Grinsell, L. V. (1934) 'Sussex Barrows', *SAC* 75, 216-275.

Hadingham, E. (1979) *Secrets of the Ice Age: The World of the Cave Artists,* Heinemann.

Megaw, J. V. S. and Simpson, D. D. A. (1979) *Introduction to British Prehistory*, Leicester University Press.

Renfrew, C. (1974) *British Prehistory*, Duckworth.

Toms, H. S. (1922) 'Long Barrows in Sussex', *SAC* 63, 157-165.

Chapter 9: Gateways for the God

Burgess, C. (1980) *The Age of Stonehenge*, Dent.

Burl, A. (1976) *The Stone Circles of the British Isles*, Yale University Press.

Curwen, E. C. (1923) 'Blackpatch Flint-Mine Excavation, 1922', *SAC* 65, 69-111.

Curwen, E. C. (1928) 'The Antiquities of Windover Hill', *SAC* 69, 93-101.

Curwen, E. C. (1934) *The Archaeology of Sussex*, Methuen.

Curwen, E. C. (1936) 'Excavation in Whitehawk Camp, Brighton', *SAC* 77, 60-92.

Drewett, P. (1977) 'The Excavation of a Neolithic Causewayed Enclosure on Offham Hill, East Sussex, 1976', Proc. Prehist. Soc. 43, 201-241.

Dyer, J. (1973) *Southern England: An Archaeological Guide*, Faber and Faber.

Furneaux, R. (1976) *Ancient Mysteries*, White Lion.

Gimbutas, M. (1974) *The Gods and Goddesses of Old Europe, 7000-3500 BC*, Thames and Hudson.

Hadingham, E. (1975) *Circles and Standing Stones*, Heinemann.

Jessup, R. (1970) *South East England*, Thames and Hudson.

Jones, I. (1655) *The Most Notable Antiquity of Great Britain, Vulgarly Called Stone-heng, Restored.*

Limbrey, S. and Evans, J. G. (ed.) (1978) *The Effect of Man on the Landscape: The Lowland Zone*, Council for British Archaeology.

Margary, I. D. (1965) *Roman Ways in the Weald*, Phoenix House.

Megaw, J. V. S. and Simpson, D. D. A. (1979) *Introduction to British Prehistory*, Leicester University Press.

Musson, R. (1950) 'An Excavation at Combe Hill Camp near Eastbourne', *SAC* 89, 105-116.

Turner, E. (1849) 'On the Military Earthworks of the South Downs', *SAC* 3, 173-184.

Williamson, R. P. R. (1930) 'Excavations in Whitehawk Neolithic Camp, near Brighton', *SAC* 71, 57-96.

Chapter 10: The Harvest Hill

Allcroft, A. H. (1922) *SAC* 63, 174-179.

Anon. (1922) 'Mounts at Lewes and Ringmer', *SAC* 63, 223-226.

Burgess, C. (1980) *The Age of Stonehenge*, Dent.

Burl, A. (1979) *Prehistoric Avebury*, Yale University Press.

Curwen, E. C. (1929) 'Excavations in the Trundle, Goodwood', *SAC* 70, 33-85.

Dames, M. (1976) *The Silbury Treasure*, Thames and Hudson.

Hope, W. H. St J. (1904) 'The Cluniac Priory of St Pancras at Lewes', *SAC* 49, 66-88.

Macleod, D. (1939) 'The Priory Mounts of Lewes and Christchurch', *SAC* 5, 228-229.

Pyatt, E. C. (1972) *Chalkways of South and South-east England*, David and Charles.

Salzman, L. F. (1922) 'The Castle of Lewes', *SAC* 63, 166-174.

Chapter 11: The Timepiece of the Green King

Forde, C. D. (1934) *Habitat, Economy and Society*, Methuen.

Hadingham, E. (1975) *Circles and Standing Stones*, Heinemann.

Hawkins, G. S. (1966) *Stonehenge Decoded*, Souvenir Press.

Chapter 12: The Guardian-God

Campbell, J. (1959) *The Masks of God*, Secker and Warburg.

Dames, M. (1976) *The Silbury Treasure*, Thames and Hudson.

Gimbutas, M. (1974) *The Gods and Goddesses of Old Europe, 7000-3500 BC*, Thames and Hudson.

Graves, R. (1948) *The White Goddess*, Faber and Faber.

Graves, R. (1960) *The Greek Myths*, Pelican.

Hadingham, E. (1979) *Secrets of the Ice Age*, Heinemann.

Harding, D. (1978) *Prehistoric Europe*, Elsevier-Phaidon.

Hudson, W. H. (1942) *Nature in Downland*, Dent.

Jung, C. G. (1956) *Symbols of Transformation*, Routledge and Kegan Paul.

Jung, C. G. (1960) *The Structure and Dynamics of the Psyche*, Routledge and Kegan Paul.

Jung, C. G. (1968) *The Archetypes and the Collective Unconscious*, Routledge and Kegan Paul.

Steinthal, H. (1861) 'Die Sage von Simson', *Zeit. für Völkerpsych*, 2, 129-178.

INDEX